How to Read Thai

by Russ Crowley & Duangta Wanthong Mondi

Published by Russ Crowley

How to Read Thai

www.howtoreadthai.com
www.learnthaialphabet.com

ISBN 978-1-908203-07-6 (colour)
ISBN 978-1-908203-12-0 (black text)
ISBN 978-1-908203-08-3 (pdf)

Translated by Duangta Wanthong Mondi.

Read What Others Have Said About Our Products

I have achieved more than I would have thought possible in such a short space of time. Your colour code and picture aids make learning so much easier and it's so easy to refresh my memory from your app. I must say Russ, for me your product has been a great help, well worth the small price paid, and, would wholeheartedly recommend it to anyone wanting to learn to read and write Thai.

Orville Earle, London, UK, 17th October 2013

The Thai language is very intimidating and this program has taken the fear away! I would give it an 11 out of 10 points!! Thanks Russ!

Sandra Ching, Ecuador, 9th September 2013

I agree that your app and those posts are like a speed-of-light catalyst in terms teaching one the Thai script and reading it within literally two days (in my experience) which I find extraordinary!... I am just extremely excited that I have finally found material that does not throw one into the deep end of things.

Emiliusz Smorczewski, Illinois, USA, 9th July 2013

I have been very pleased with how quickly I have been able to learn and retain so much. Another aspect to purchasing is the quality of service received. The iPad version is awesome because I can use it anywhere without internet. I travel a lot and often am without internet, so it makes it nice.

Brian Atwell, USA, 3rd October 2013

Your book made learning the pronunciation and alphabet very easy. Thanks again.

Allen Mitchell, 9th April 2013

Your teaching technique is very good, much better than the other books I've seen.

Julian Wheeler, Chonburi, Thailand, 28th October 2012

This is the best help I've had, thank you so much, really easy to understand.

Rebekah Wilkes, UK, 7th May 2013

I'm surprised at how quickly and easily this is all sinking in. Thanks for making it easy.

Mitch Costello, Sydney, Australia, 9th September 2013

These resources are making the learning of Thai a reality after numerous false starts... the simplicity of the system breaks down the psychological barriers to attacking the idea of reading/writing Thai.

Brock Estes, Richmond, VA, 15th September 2012

How to Read Thai - Colour v Black Text

There are two versions of this book: one colour (ISBN 78-1-908203-11-3), and one non-colour (black text only - ISBN 978-1-908203-12-0); we also have the colour version in pdf available from the website, below. Following a survey of existing customers, we chose to publish both due to: 1) interest; and, 2) the vast difference in printing costs between colour and black versions.

Is the Colour Version Necessary?

Our system uses colour throughout and we continue the theme in the colour version. If you've bought **Learning Thai Your Great Adventure**, **Memory Aids to Your Great Adventure**, and **The Learn Thai Alphabet application**, then you'll be very familiar with the simple colour-code (plus naming conventions, transliteration, acronyms, etc,) we use and we apply this to our read Thai system to help you visualise and follow exactly what we're talking about.

If you know the Thai alphabet, then maybe you'll be comfortable without the colour system; but, if you're unsure, then purely because of printing costs, it is going to cost more.

Does this Book Teach Me the Thai Alphabet?

No it doesn't. Naturally, we have the full tables of consonants and vowels, but this isn't teaching. If you want to learn the alphabet, we've created **The Learn Thai Alphabet application** (for web and iPad 2+) and **Memory Aids to Your Great Adventure** (the book version). Both of these will teach you the alphabet quickly and get you to the starting point necessary for this book. If you don't know the Thai alphabet yet, this book isn't going to be of much use until you do.

Learn the
Thai Alphabet
on your pc, Mac,
and iPad!

www.learnthaialphabet.com

How to Read Thai

Simple Vowels

Complex Vowels

Reading Strategies and Texts

Appendices

How to Read Thai

Getting Started

Welcome to **QuEST: Quick, Easy, Simple Thai** and our **How to Read Thai** book. As far as we're aware, this is the first book of its kind that covers the step-by-step process of actually reading Thai script.

There are a number of books available that claim to teach you to read Thai, but most just explain the Thai alphabet to you and consider that to be reading Thai. Yes, they may give you some other information such as words or sentences in different fonts and such like, but that isn't actually helping you a great deal.

Having said that, there are some that don't even do that, they just give you a list of consonants, a list of vowels, some basic Thai words, a short explanation about consonant classes, a table or two about tone marks and calculating tone, and then some Thai script. According to them, you can now read Thai.

However, the problem is, we both know that though this may work for a few select individuals (we're all different, right?), for the vast majority this isn't that beneficial. Also, it doesn't actually tell or teach you how to read Thai script. Sure, it may help you learn the alphabet and a few of the rules for calculating the correct tone but it's not teaching you to read Thai. I'll be honest with you here, learning the Thai alphabet is one thing, but learning to read is another.

Learning the Thai Alphabet

Yes, you have to learn the alphabet to be able to read Thai. If you don't know the alphabet, then please put this book down and, as we have said before, look at getting either our **Memory Aids to Your Great Adventure** book, or our web and iPad application, **The Learn Thai Alphabet application**: both of which are excellent resources and help you to quickly learn all the required elements of the Thai alphabet. Once you've learnt the alphabet - or at the very least the consonants - then you can start learning to read Thai.

If you start trying to read before you know the alphabet then it's going to be slow and confusing. Also, just to clarify, when we say '*You must know the alphabet*', we mean that you can recognise each consonant, you know the initial and final consonant sound(s), and you know the consonant class. If you don't, then this will make the learning process harder and slower until you get up to speed. In addition, you also need to be able to recognise each vowel, know the vowel sounds, and what the difference is between a short and a long vowel.

If you're about 50% of the way there, or have purchased this book with a view to learning the alphabet first and then using this book, that's also fine; but, just as long as you understand that you have to know certain things before you move onto the next step. Until you're proficient, then your progress will be hindered because of it.

Just to clarify, you don't need to know the actual Thai names of the consonants or their meaning at this step, you can learn these at your leisure later on; perhaps after you're up to speed with reading and your confidence is on the rise.

The Quest System - Quick, Easy, Simple, Thai

The good thing for you is *Quest: Quick, Easy, Simple Thai* makes learning the alphabet so easy and fast. Again, our recommendation is if you don't know the alphabet 100%, then we'd advise you to invest in the book or the application and save yourself a considerable amount of time and effort.

With *Quest*, we use the same transliterated text, the same picture-consonant-vowel names, the same tone acronyms and so on throughout this book (and all our materials), to ensure that learning is **Qu**ick, **E**asy, and **S**imple (**T**hai). This level of consistency ensures you only have to learn one system and one system alone. If you're new to learning Thai you may be asking why this is important?

One System

Well, when you consider there are 12 different transliteration systems in use in Thailand, no-one realistically wants to learn all of them; what's the point? Similarly, if your goal is to read Thai script, then learning just one transliterated system is still one-too-many; but, we all know we've got to start somewhere and, because of that, the sooner we can get rid of the transliteration the better. As such, why bother learning multiple systems? We want to get by with one system and get to the point where we no longer need it as quickly as we can.

Using *Quest* ensures you use **just one system** and, as your time is being used more effectively, you know you are progressing towards your goal of learning to read Thai.

How is this Book Different?

Delivering or teaching content to different students and audiences requires a flexible approach and, where complex processes are involved, to ensure everyone understands exactly what is going on, the first thing to do is often to simplify everything by breaking these down into easily manageable steps.

This is particularly important when teaching via non face-to-face methods such as a book. If it's not explained correctly, then the reader has no recourse for questioning and can get easily stuck. Simple is always best.

You probably realise that we can apply this simplification to practically every aspect of our daily lives; and, when we have a subject about which we know very little, we also need sufficient detail otherwise there is real risk of over-simplification and the information that we do give is maybe insufficient to do the actual job.

Okay, you may know the Thai alphabet and it's also quite possible that you may have quite a varied range of vocabulary, but how do you apply what you've learned to breaking a complete sentence down, identifying the sylla-bles, the words, and actually reading it? Unless you can apply some order, sense, or logic to this unfamiliar script, then what you know is of limited value. As you probably realise, learning the Thai alphabet is merely the first step in the process.

What you need to be able to do is apply this knowledge in the correct way. Sure, you can probably muddle through, it just takes time. This is what Russ had to do as there weren't any books to explain this. But, in this book we describe the actual processes to deconstruct sentences into words and words into syllables – exactly what you need to start learning to read Thai. This is what makes our book different.

No other book gives you this level of detail; a level of detail which GUARAN-TEES that by the end **you will be able to read Thai**.

Using This Book

As we go through the book, we cover the sounds, both initial and final, in great detail; and, you can see how, why, and when each are used. This way you can see exactly what each initial consonant, vowel, and final consonant is doing.

For the first 8-10 chapters (to about page 151), so you get to experience hands-on the structure of this book, and how we approach this topic, we introduce single and multi-syllable words and move onto sample sentences so you get a feel for how they are constructed. Then, as we progress, these get gradually more complex when, towards the end of the book, we introduce some short paragraphs (at various levels to give you an indication of where you currently are).

What Level Are You Currently At?

Regardless of your level, we'd recommend that you don't skip parts in this book as we're confident that there is material here which hasn't been explained before in other books or websites which you may have seen. If it turns out you do know most of this, then it'll act as a refresher and familiarise you with our terminology.

Once again though, **this book is not designed to teach you the Thai alphabet**. The assumption is that you have already achieved, or are well on the way to achieving, that level of ability.

If you think you can get by with this book without knowing our system, then if *galahad knight, wave over, squirrel tail, steeple*, or *reindeer* mean nothing to you, then there is a chance you may be confused. These are the names we use to refer to the consonants and vowels and they contain the initial and final consonant sounds, and vowel sounds, respectively.

If you're not 100% there, or are unsure, then check out our other products (page 370); and, these will certainly help clarify all of this and bridge the gap between what you currently know and what you must know.

As Brock kindly says:

> *"…I highly recommend the books and the App and the invest-*
> *ment in the time to do those early enough in your learning of*
> *Thai; since I think it will make a tremendous difference in how*
> *quickly and how much of the language you pick up as time goes*
> *on, regardless of what methods you use in learning the spoken*
> *language."*

> *Brock Estes, Richmond Virginia, 15th September 2013.*

Layout

We introduce you to our system straightaway. We use colour extensively to distinguish between consonant and vowels, and consonant classes within the former category. If you have paid extra and have the colour book then this will all fall into place easily; if you don't have a colour version, then it's going to be plain old bold text for you. Don't worry, you can still get there, it's just **Quest** is designed *end-to-end* and if you learn with our single colour system, then you'll be in a better position as a result. Regardless, we use the first set of chapters to concentrate on single and multi-syllable words.

You will come across the term 'compound words' a lot when we talk about words with two or more syllables. This is because unless we have a wide vocabulary and a good knowledge of the language, it's unlikely that we would know if a word is in its base form, is derivational, inflectional, an idiom, etc. Admittedly, some are obvious, but many aren't; and, we believe it helps to stay consistent.

In the chapter entitled สระ เ-า (page 147), we start to introduce sentences with each example; and, with these sentences we elaborate on grammar where needed. This isn't a grammar book by any stretch of the imagination, so we don't go overboard on this subject. As you can imagine, entire books have been written on that particular topic and if you do have a passion or a penchant for grammar, we have listed the grammar resources we ourselves use in our Thai Grammar Resources section (page 340).

Following on from this, we then start to phase out the more common consonant names and sounds: we use the very common names such as *galahad knight, dog treat,* and *navigation* for remembering the shape and the sounds of the consonants (refer to *Memory Aids to Your Great Adventure*) extensively at first, and by the time you get to that point, you should know automatically that ก makes the /**g**/ sound as an initial consonant, and /**k**/ when it's in the final position.

We then make a few more alterations so that by the time you reach the end of the book we will be purely using proper Thai script with no colour coding and no picture names – you now know *How to Read Thai.*

Our Products

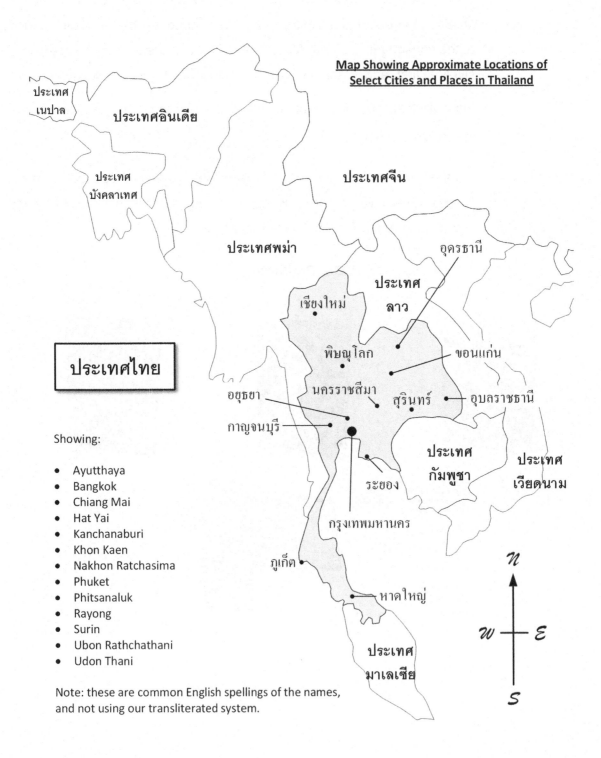

**Map Showing Approximate Locations of
Select Cities and Places in Thailand**

ประเทศ
เนปาล

ประเทศอินเดีย

ประเทศ
บังคลาเทศ

ประเทศจีน

ประเทศพม่า

อุดรธานี

ประเทศ
ลาว

เชียงใหม่

พิษณุโลก

ขอนแก่น

ประเทศไทย

นครราชสีมา

สุรินทร์

อุบลราชธานี

อยุธยา

กาญจนบุรี

ประเทศ
กัมพูชา

ประเทศ
เวียดนาม

ระยอง

กรุงเทพมหานคร

ภูเก็ต

หาดใหญ่

ประเทศ
มาเลเซีย

Showing:

- Ayutthaya
- Bangkok
- Chiang Mai
- Hat Yai
- Kanchanaburi
- Khon Kaen
- Nakhon Ratchasima
- Phuket
- Phitsanaluk
- Rayong
- Surin
- Ubon Rathchathani
- Udon Thani

Note: these are common English spellings of the names,
and not using our transliterated system.

N

W E

S

The Thai Alphabet

About the Thai Alphabet

The Thai alphabet consists of 44 consonants and 32 vowels. With an unfamiliar script, no spaces between words, few spaces between sentences, and minimal punctuation, learning to read Thai can be a daunting prospect for many.

Dispelling this myth is one of the primary reasons we've written this book and together we can take you from the beginning stages through to being able to read Thai. Just to be sure, by the end of this book you will be able to read and understand a simple elementary-level short story written in Thai script by a native Thai.

However, though that's just the basics, you will then be equipped with everything you need to read Thai and we will have provided you with the knowledge and ability to deconstruct sentences into their component parts and to be able to read and understand each word.

Levels of Language

You may, or may not know this, but we use different levels of language in our daily lives whether at home or abroad; and Thai and Thailand are no different.

For example, we use what could be considered a day-to-day language when we talk with friends and family, whereas this will be different to that used in your workplace and with your boss at work. Similarly, the language used in a work environment would be markedly different to that used to converse with royalty or monks, who use a select higher level of language. Of course, all of these verbal interactions are markedly different from that we see in written texts.

To illustrate this, consider the language used in a novel against that used in an academic or scientific paper. What if you compare the level of language used in, say, a broad-sheet newspaper with that used in a daily 'rag', which typically use a lot of abbreviations and slang, and you will get an idea of the difficulties in reading different publications.

A daily newspaper is particularly difficult for a non-native beginner to grasp and requires a higher level of language knowledge and reading ability than, let's say, a short story which uses fairly basic language.

In addition, you have to appreciate that though written Thai is quite phonetic, there are a number exceptions to the normal spelling (and pronunciation) rules which, as a learner, you just have to commit to memory.

What we try and stick to is simpler texts to get you started, to build your knowledge, your ability, your confidence, and to get you to this basic level of language by the end of the book. When you have achieved this level of reading you will be equipped with a solid, sound foundation upon which to progress to a higher level or ability. Then, as they say, the rest is up to you.

Transliteration System

As we've already said, we always recommend that you do away with transliterated script at the earliest opportunity and start learning to read Thai script; of course, this is probably the very reason you have this book.

Nevertheless, transliterated script does play its part, and we use it for the first half of the book in order that you can follow along with exactly where we are and what we're talking about.

As in all our material, we use the **Paiboon system** whereby single vowels are represented by a short vowel: /**a**/, /**e**/, /**i**/, etc., and long vowels are distinguishable by doubling-up on the vowel: /**aa**/, /**ee**/, /**ii**/, and so on.[1] This is an instant, easy to see, and clear method of distinguishing between vowel lengths, which you have to know to pronounce the length and tone of the words correctly.

The Paiboon system also uses written tone marks to represent syllable and word tone. There are 5 tones in Thai, and every syllable or word must have one of these tones, these are:

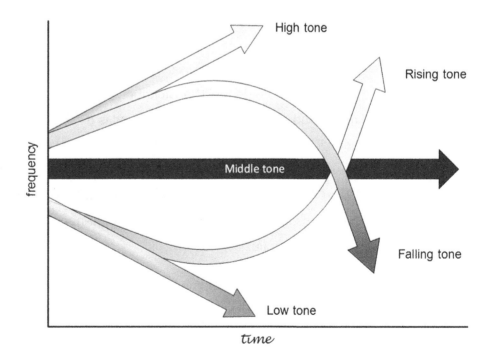

Figure 1 - The 5 Tones in Thai

---

1. There are many more elements to the Paiboon and Paiboon+ system including word stress and tone but we only want to use it as a stepping-stone, not as a language system.

Table 1 shows the 4 tone signs that are used in transliterated Thai. These signs are different to the tone marks used in Thai script. We cover the Thai tone marks in "Tone Marks" on page 28:

Table 1. Transliterated Tone Signs

Tone	Tone Sign	Example	You say it with…
Middle	No tone sign	Gaa	…your normal voice, constant pitch.
Low	\	Gàa	…your voice starting at a slightly lower pitch than your normal (mid tone) voice, dropping, and finishing lower.
Falling	^	Gâa	…your voice starting higher than your mid tone, rising, and then dropping, finally finishing lower than mid tone.
High	/	Gáa	…your voice starting higher than mid tone, rising, and finishing higher.
Rising	v	Gǎa	…your voice starting lower than your mid tone, dropping, and then rising, finally finishing higher than mid tone.

Consonants

Table 2 shows a complete lists of Thai consonants, all 44 of them. It also shows their order in the Thai alphabet; the initial consonant sound they make; and, if the final consonant sound is different to the initial consonant sound, this also. The fifth column is headed 'Picture Name', and this corresponds to the easy to remember pictures we use in **Memory Aids to Your Great Adventure** and in **The Learn Thai Alphabet application**. The consonant class for each consonant is in the right-hand column, you need to know this, it is essential.

For those unfamiliar with the **Quest** system, we bold letters to indicate the sounds made. For those consonants whose 'picture name' is a single word description, e.g. **k**angaroo, the bold letter identifies the sound that this consonant makes (the /**k**/ sound) regardless of whether it's an initial, medial, or final consonant position in a syllable or word.

For those pictures with two-word descriptions, such as **g**alahad **k**night, or **ch**ef **t**asting, the initial consonant sound is indicated by the bold consonant (or consonants if 2 letters are selected) of the first word, and the medial or a final consonant sound is indicated by the bold consonant(s) of the second word.

With the exception of the number and the actual consonant name, you need to know all of the information in this table (and you <u>must</u> know it all if you want to read Thai). Again, we refer to these sounds and picture names extensively in this book.

Table 2. **List of Consonants and Sounds**

No.	Consonant Name	Initial Conso-nant Sound	Final Consonant Sound	As in (picture name)	Class (H, M, L)
1	ก ไก่	/g/	/k/	**g**alahad **k**night [a]	Middle
2	ข ไข่	/k/		**k**angaroo	High
3	ฃ ขวด	/k/		**k**araoke	High
4	ค ควาย	/k/		**k**oala	Low
5	ฅ คน	/k/		**k**oala	Low
6	ฆ ระฆัง	/k/		**k**ite	Low
7	ง งู	/ng/		guardi**ng**	Low
8	จ จาน	/j/	/t/	**j**abberwocky **t**ail	Middle
9	ฉ ฉิ่ง	/ch/	/t/	**ch**at's **t**ail	High
10	ช ช้าง	/ch/	/t/	**ch**ef **t**asting	Low
11	ซ โซ่	/s/	/t/	**s**axophone **t**wins	Low
12	ฌ เฌอ	/ch/	/t/	**ch**ild **t**antrum	Low
13	ญ หญิง	/y/	/n/	**y**ou're **n**icked	Low
14	ฎ ชฎา	/d/	/t/	**d**og **t**reat	Middle
15	ฏ ปฏัก	/dt/	/t/	**d**og **t**reat	Middle
16	ฐ ฐาน	/t/		**t**assles	High
17	ฑ มณโฑ	/t/		**t**ortoise	Low
18	ฒ ผู้เฒ่า	/t/		**t**raining	Low
19	ณ เณร	/n/		**n**apoleon	Low
20	ด เด็ก	/d/	/t/	**d**amsel **t**ower	Middle

Table 2. List of Consonants and Sounds

21	ต เต่า	/dt/ [b]	/t/	damsel tower	Middle
22	ถ ถุง	/t/		tails	High
23	ท ทหาร	/t/		typist	Low
24	ธ ธง	/t/		tea-bag	Low
25	น หนู	/n/		navigating	Low
26	บ ใบไม้	/b/	/p/	bald patch	Middle
27	ป ปลา	/bp/	/p/	bottom pit	Middle
28	ผ ผึ้ง	/p/		profits	High
29	ฝ ฝา	/f/	/p/	fruit picking	High
30	พ พาน	/p/		praying	Low
31	ฟ ฟัน	/f/	/p/	finished picking	Low
32	ภ สำเภา	/p/		painting	Low
33	ม ม้า	/m/		map	Low
34	ย ยักษ์	/y/	/i/	yeti ice	Low
36	ร เรือ	/r/	/n/	rabbit nibbling	Low
36	ล ลิง	/l/	/n/	large nugget	Low
37	ว แหวน	/w/	/o/	wave over	Low
38	ศ ศาลา	/s/	/t/	sign top	High
39	ษ ฤๅษี	/s/	/t/	sea trip	High
40	ส เสือ	/s/	/t/	squirrel tail	High
41	ห หีบ	/h/		humps	High
42	ฬ จุฬา	/l/	/n/	looking nice	Low
43	อ อ่าง	/ɔɔ/		awful [weather]	Middle
44	ฮ นกฮูก	/h/		hooray	Low

a. The final consonant sound for ก ไก่ is the hard /k/ sound. Russ is a big Monty Python fan, and this represents the "kerrr-nigget" sound, rather than the traditional pronunciation of the word knight.

b. The sounds /**dt**/ and /**bp**/ have no direct equivalent in the English language as an *initial sound*, but, make sounds similar to the '**t**' as it /stop/, and the '**p**' as in /spend/.

Note: *we have omitted some information from this table. If you are a beginner, then you don't need to know the actual Thai consonant name at this stage. Later on, yes; but, now it'll delay you. However, if you wish to learn the proper names as you go, the full table is in Appendix A - Full List of Thai Consonants on page 328.*

Consonant Classes

Every consonant belongs to one of three classes: High, Middle or Low. A consonant's class never changes. The function of the consonant class it to help determine syllable and word tone.

With our colour-coding system, we use red, yellow, and green to denote High, Middle, and Low class. If you think of a traffic light, you'll be able to picture them easily.

Special consonants

There are 2 consonants that have more than one role within Thai: **M**iddle Class อ อ่าง (**a**wful weather) and High Class ห หีบ (**h**umps). These multi-roles are concerned with tone and pronunciation so rather than locate them here, you can find them in "Multi-Role Consonants" on page 32.

Consonant Clusters

Consonant clusters are treated as a single consonant.

A consonant cluster is where two consonants are joined together to form a particular sound. **Consonant clusters are treated as one consonant**. Important to note is there is no unwritten vowel between consonants in a cluster and both consonants are spoken.

An example in English is /**spend**/. The /**sp**/ is a consonant cluster and means the consonants are pronounced together to give the word /**spend**/ (and not /**sa-pend**/).

With consonant clusters, vowels are always written above or below the **second** consonant in the cluster.

As shown in Table 3, there are only 5 initial consonant sounds for consonant clusters:

Recognising Consonant Clusters

can be one of the biggest problems for beginners learning to break down sentences and words.

They are very common so please learn them.

Table 3. **The 5 Initial Consonant Cluster Sounds**

Initial Consonant(s)	Sound
ก	/**g**/
ข and ค	/**k**/
ต	/**dt**/
ป	/**bp**/
ผ and พ	/**p**/

The second consonant in a cluster will always be either:

ร (Rɔɔ Rʉʉa), ล (Lɔɔ Ling) or ว (Wɔɔ Wɛ̆ɛn)

Consonant Clusters

*always begin with /**g**/, /**k**/, /**dt**/, /**bp**/ or /**p**/.*

(ก, ข, ค, ต, ป, ผ, or พ)

*The second consonant is **always** /**r**/, /**l**/, or /**w**/*

(ร, ล, or ว)

Table 4 shows the complete list of consonant clusters and includes some examples:

Table 4. List of Consonant Clusters

Cluster	Pronunciation	Example
กร-	/gr/	โกรธ (gròot - *angry, mad*)
กล-	/gl/	กลับ (glàp - *return, go back*)
กว-	/gw/	กว่า (gwàa - *more*)
ขร-	/kr/	ขรึม (krŭm - *serious*)
ขล-	/kl/	ขลุ่ย (klùi - *flute*)
ขว-	/kw/	ขวา (kwăa - *right*)
คร-	/kr/	ครับ (kráp - *polite particle used by males*)
คล-	/k/	โคลง (kloong - *poem, poetry*)
คว-	/kw/	ความ (kwaam - *a prefix that converts a verb or an adjective into a noun*)
ตร-	/dtr/	ตรง (dtrong - *at, straight*)
ปร-	/bpr/	ประเทศ (bprà-têet - *country, nation*)
ปล-	/bpl/	ปลา (bplaa - *fish*)
ผล-	/p/	ผลัก (plàk - *push, shove*)
พร-	/pr/	พระ (prá - *buddha image or statue*)
พล-	/pl/	พลิก (plík - *turn over*)

Vowels and tone marks are written above the second consonant in a consonant cluster.

Remember, when using clusters they are considered to be one consonant; and, when a vowel or a tone mark is written above or below a cluster, it is written above or below the second consonant in that cluster (as shown in many examples in Table 3, including: พลิก, ผลัก, ครับ, and กลับ).

Vowels

There are 32 vowels in the Thai alphabet and they are divided into 2 categories: simple and complex. Unlike consonants, vowels have no class; but, this isn't meant to say they are uncouth or aren't great, it's just they don't operate in the same way that consonants do.

Every syllable must have a vowel.

Every syllable in Thai **must have** a **vowel**. We'll just repeat this so we're sure: every syllable <u>must have</u> a vowel, This is unlike English where every syllable must have a **vowel sound** (think of the word *rhythm*).

Simple and complex vowels are also sub-divided into two other categories: short vowels and long vowels.

As we mentioned earlier, with the Paiboon system short vowels have a single letter and long vowels have a double letter: this makes identifying the difference in vowel length simple, instant, and unambiguous, e.g. /**a**/ for a short vowel, and /**aa**/ for a long vowel.

The vowel length is important for calculating tone and correct pronunciation.

The following section will provide you with a refresher on the vowels, the sounds, and the picture names we use within *Quest* (a full list of vowels is in Appendix B on page 330).

Simple Vowels

There are 20 simple vowels. Unlike in English, vowels in Thai always makes the same sound regardless of where the vowel is written or what consonant it is written with.

If you think of the vowel 'a' in English, you realise it can make lots of different sounds depending on where in the word, and with which other letters, it is written. For example, for the letter 'a' we have *cap, tuna* (short sound), *yacht, boat, sail, roar, many, anchor<u>a</u>ge, weather;* so that's 9 different sounds (including compound vowels) from just that one vowel. Thai is much easier in this respect. Table 5 shows the full list of simple vowels:

Table 5. **Full List of Simple Vowels**

Short Vowel			Long Vowel		
Vowel	**Sound**	**Sounds Like**	**Vowel**	**Sound**	**Sounds Like**
			-ํา	/am/	**um**brella
The 4 vowels to the right can be short or long but are considered long for tone purposes.			ใ-	/ai/	knight
			ไ-	/ai/	fly
			เ-า	/ao/	mo**u**se
-ะ	/a/	puffin	-า	/aa/	palm
-ิ	/i/	lip	-ี	/ii/	steeple
-ึ	/ʉ/	push-up	-ื	/ʉʉ/	bloom
-ุ	/u/	crook	-ู	/uu/	boot
เ-ะ	/e/	net	เ-	/ee/	bed
แ-ะ	/ɛ/	trap	แ-	/ɛɛ/	mare
โ-ะ	/o/	cot	โ-	/oo/	ghost
เ-าะ	/ɔ/	slot	-อ	/ɔɔ/	**aw**ful

If you look at the long vowel on the last row, you may also recognise this as being the 43rd consonant (อ อ่าง) – it is; yes, and just to confuse matters, this particular consonant can also be a vowel. Don't fret though, we cover this in great detail in "Multi-Role Consonants" starting on page 32.

Complex Vowels

There are 12 complex vowels. Eight of them are in common use but the remaining four are extremely rare. These 4 are the first four short vowels as shown by the shaded area in Table 6 (we cover all vowels in detail later on).

Table 6. **Full List of Complex Vowels**

Short Vowel			Long Vowel		
Vowel	Sound	Sounds Like	Vowel	Sound	Sounds Like
เ-อะ	/ə/	above	เ-อ	/əə/	early
เ-ียะ	/ia/	ria	เ-ีย	/iia/	reindeer
เ-ือะ	/ʉa/	newer	เ-ือ	/ʉʉa/	skua
-ัวะ	/ua/	buat	-ัว	/uua/	pure
ฤ	/rʉ/	rook	ฤๅ	/rʉʉ/	root
ฦ	/lʉ/	look-out	ฦๅ	/lʉʉ/	looney

The Inherent Vowel

Every consonant in Thai has an *inherent* vowel. This inherent vowel is สระ -อ. It is inherent, it is invisible, and is always spoken.

Why Do We Need The Inherent Vowel?

Remember, there are 5 consonants in Thai that make the /**k**/ sound as an initial consonant, and 4 that make the /**s**/ sound as an initial consonant; plus, when you consider the **p**'s, the **n**'s, and the **t**'s, it can get confusing. Naturally, there has to be a way to distinguish between consonants.

To do this, each consonant is given a name. For example, the full name of the first letter of the Thai alphabet (ก) is ก ไก่. This name consists of 2 parts: the first part of the consonant name (ก) is the sound the consonant makes as an initial consonant; and, the second part of the consonant name (ไก่) is the noun after which it is named - its *distinguishing name*. The word ไก่ means *chicken*. So the consonant name ก ไก่ is associated with, or named after, a *chicken*.

If we spell ก ไก่ out in transliterated Thai, we would write /**gɔɔ gài**/. We can see where the /**gài**/ came from: สระ ไ- gives us the /**ai**/ as in *fly* sound; and in our *Quest system,* the ก gives us the /**g**/ as in *galahad knight* sound; but, where did the /**ɔɔ**/ part of /**gɔɔ**/ come from?

The Inherent Vowel

The inherent vowel makes the /ɔɔ/ as in awful sound.

Well, let's see what it looks like if we don't have the /**ɔɔ**/ (inherent vowel) sound. We'll get rid of it so the name is now /**g gài**/ which, if you say it out loud - I think you'll agree - sounds both guttural and horrible, and is not something you'd particularly want to refer to. To our knowledge, this is the reason why every consonant has the inherent vowel /**ɔɔ**/.

The inherent vowel is considered part of the consonant name, is never written out (unless you use transliterated script), and is always pronounced when spelling, or referring to the consonant, e.g. ง งู is always called /**ngɔɔ nguu**/, ป ปลา is always called /**bpɔɔ bplaa**/, and ส เสือ is always /**sɔɔ suua**/.

A full list of consonants and their Thai names is in Appendix A on page 328.

Where to Write Vowels

In Thai, vowels can be written before, above, after, and below consonants. This may seem quite daunting due to its unfamiliarity, but that's all it is – unfamiliarity. We can assure you that you will quickly learn where they are written.

This is vital as though you have to know where to write all vowels, all vowels have 'rules' associated with them; and, knowing these rules helps us identify where the syllable and word breaks are. As you can imagine, in a script where there are no word breaks, this is essential knowledge.

Just so we're clear, when we write vowels, the dash (-), or the vowel place-holder (อ) indicates where the consonant is written in relation to the vowel (or where the vowel is in relation to the consonant - this **never** changes). They are used interchangeably but they mean the same thing: so when you see -า written, it is the same as us writing อา to indicate placement.

Vowels Before

Table 7 shows the vowels that are always written before an **initial** consonant:

Table 7. Vowels Written Before Consonants

Vowels Before	Examples
ไ-	ไก่ ไข่ ไหม ไทย ไก่ย่าง
ใ-	ใช่ ใคร ใบ สะใภ้
โ-	โรง โต โสด
เ-	เป็น เน้น เย็น
แ-	แล แล้ว แล้วแต่

Vowels Above

Table 8 shows the vowels that are always written above an **initial** consonant:

Table 8. **Vowels Written Above Consonants**

Initial Consonants
Vowels written above and below are always written above initial consonants.

Vowels Above	Examples
◌ิ	คิด สิ่ง ปิด
◌ี	กี่ ขี่ นี่ มี
◌ึ	ดึง ยึด บึกบึน
◌ื	มือ ทื่อ พื้น

Vowels After

Table 9 shows the vowels that are always written after a consonant:

Table 9. **Vowels Written After Consonants**

Vowels After	Examples
◌ำ	ทำ กำลัง ประจำปี
◌ะ	จะ ค่ะ กะปิ
◌า	รา กา จาก การ

Vowels Below

As shown in Table 10, there are only two vowels in Thai that are written below **initial** consonants:

Table 10. **Vowels Written below Consonants**

Vowels Below	Examples
◌ุ	คุณ คุย คลุม
◌ู	กุ้ง งู ดู รู้

Sounds

Table 2 on page 13 shows us the initial and final consonant sounds that each consonant makes. This is important to know for correct pronunciation.

For example, near where Russ used to live in the UK, there was a Thai restaurant called 'Sawasdee' (this is written in Thai script as สวัสดี). You may also have heard this word being pronounced sà-wàt-dii.

The only difference is between the pronunciation of **s** and the **t** at the end of the second syllable.

In the Paiboon transliterated system (and one or two others for that matter) the consonant ส has an initial consonant sound /s/, and a final consonant sound /t/ (as in *squirrel tail* in Quest). The first ส is in the initial consonant position, the second ส is in the final position, and the discrepancy in pronunciation and tone is due to changing this final sound.

Final Consonant Sounds

In Thai, though there are a total of 21 **initial consonant sounds**, there are only 8 **final consonant sounds**. These 8 final[2] consonant sounds are:

/ng/ (ง), **/n/** (น), **/m/** (ม), **/i/** (ย), **/o/** (ว), **/k/** (ก), **/t/** (ด), and **/p/** (บ).

We can further sub-divide this final consonant sounds group into 2 groups by the way the sounds are actually produced: **sonorant** sounds and **stop** sounds.

---

2. We also use the word 'terminal' to describe the final consonant or final vowel position or sound - they are used interchangeably: *final* consonant position is the same as writing *terminal* consonant position; final vowel is the same as writing terminal vowel. Our *Quest system* uses the Paiboon transliteration system of /k/, /p/, and /t/ as the final consonant sounds of ก, บ, and ด.

Final Sounds
You must know if the final consonant sound is sonorant or stop.

A ***sonorant sound*** has a continuous, resonant, <u>voiced</u> sound; whereas a ***stop sound*** is a <u>voiceless</u> sound where all air (the airflow) is stopped by the vocal tract.

It is important to know whether the final sound in <u>every syllable</u> is sonorant or stop as this is one of the factors in determining syllable and word tone.

Sonorant Sounds

Sonorant Final Sounds
*There are 5: /**ng**/, /**n**/, /**m**/, /**i**/, and /**o**/*

Sonorant sounds are fully voiced and when you voice these sounds, your larynx will vibrate. Table 11 shows the consonants that make the sonorant sounds:

Table 11. Sonorant Final Sounds

Consonant	Final Sound
ง	/ng/
ญ ณ น ร ล and ฬ	/n/
ม	/m/
ย	/i/
ว	/o/

Stop Sounds

As 5 of the 8 stop final sounds are sonorant, this leaves 3 stop sounds. The 3 stop sounds are: /**k**/, /**t**/, and /**p**/.

When you say these stop sounds in full, each sound is aspirated. This means if you say each of these in turn you should feel the airflow from your mouth - try it. Put a single piece of paper in front of your mouth as you say each one: the air from your mouth should cause the paper to vibrate.

However, **all Thai stop sounds** are **unaspirated**. This means no air comes out when you pronounce the sound.

Put that same piece of paper in front of your mouth and say /**pool**/, do you feel the air? Now, with the piece of paper still in front of your mouth, say /**spool**/. You shouldn't feel any air. It's the same letter **p**, just pronounced differently. This is what you need to try and achieve when you produce these stop sounds (you may need a Thai friend to help you here).

There is a lot to learn as a beginner, and sometimes we just need something simple to jog the memory. Here's a sentence I use to help me when my brain is in pause mode:

***Stop** eating **KP** nuts as they stick in your **T**eeth.*

Table 12 shows the complete list of Thai consonants that produce the stop sounds:

Stop Final Sounds
There are 3:
/k/, /p/, and /t/

Table 12. **Stop Final Sounds**

Consonant	Final Sound
ก ข ค and ฆ	/k/
จ ฉ ช ซ ฌ ฎ ฏ ฐ ฑ ฒ ด ต ถ ท ธ ศ ษ and ส	/t/
บ ป ผ ฝ พ ฟ and ภ	/p/

Back to our example...

Referring back to our earlier example of the restaurant, if you pronounce the restaurant name as they wrote it, it would be a sonorant /**s**/ sound at the end of the second syllable; whereas, if you pronounced it as a /**t**/ stop sound, the sound would be slightly different and be pronounced correctly.

To reiterate, it is important to know which are sonorant final sounds, and which are stop final sounds as these help us determine tone. We will look at tone next.

Tone

Thai is a tonal language and every syllable has one of 5 tones:

- *high*

- *falling*

- *mid*

- *rising*

- *low*.

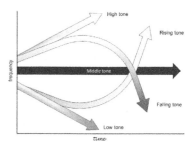

*You have to calculate the tone of **every syllable and word**.*

It would make things slightly easier if tone classification corresponded with consonant class, but it doesn't; and, unless a tone mark is present, we have to calculate the tone of **every syllable and word**.

There are 2 factors which affect the syllable tone:

1. First, if a tone mark is present this determines the tone; and, though you still need to know the consonant class of the initial consonant no other calculation is then necessary.

2. Second, if no tone mark is present, then you need to know the consonant class and whether the syllable is a live syllable or a dead syllable.

   (Also, if the consonant class is Low Class <u>and</u> the syllable is a dead syllable, then you need to know the vowel length as well).

We will address each of these in order.

Tone Marks

If a tone mark is present, then there is no need to calculate tone: <u>it overrides all other tone rules</u>. There are only 4 tone marks in Thai script, these are shown in Table 13:

Table 13. Tone Marks

Tone Mark	Name		When the tone mark is written above the following consonant class, the syllable tone will be:		
			Low Class	Middle Class	High Class
่	Mái èek	ไม้เอก	Falling tone (^)	Low tone (\)	Low tone (\)
้	Mái too	ไม้โท	High tone (/)	Falling tone (^)	Falling tone (^)
๊	Mái dtrii	ไม้ตรี	High tone (/)		
๋	Mái jat-dta-waa	ไม้จัตวา	Rising tone (v)		

Remembering Tone Marks

Learning this table and putting it into practice can be difficult; but, Table 14 shows our easy to use pictures to help you remember (these are the pictures we use in The *Learn Thai Alphabet app* and *MATGA*).

Table 14. Tone Marks the Quest Way

่	High and Middle Class consonants = *low tone* Low Class consonants = *falling tone*	
้	High and Middle Class consonants = *falling tone* Low Class consonants = *high tone*	
๊	All consonants = *high tone*	
๋	All consonants = *rising tone*	

If no tone mark is present then we must calculate tone <u>every time</u>.

Writing Tone Marks

Vowels and tone marks are written above the second consonant in a consonant cluster.

Tone marks are always written above the first consonant in a syllable or a word. This is very useful for helping us identify where a syllable or word begins. Of course, as we mentioned on page 16, a consonant cluster is considered a single consonant and, when a tone mark is written above a cluster, it is always written above the second consonant in the cluster.

Tone Calculations

There are no two ways about it, calculating tone can be a slow process. In fact, until you start learning, practicing, and finally get it off to a tee, getting it correct will slow you down. We have some acronyms to help speed this up, but first we need to show you the 'correct' way to do it.

Calculating Tone

1. Consonant class
2. Live or dead syllable
3. If Low class, then long or short vowel.

To calculate tone, you need to know the following:

1. What the class of the **initial consonant** is.

2. Whether the syllable is **live** or **dead**?

3. Also, if the consonant class is Low Class <u>and</u> the syllable is a dead syllable, then you also need to know whether the vowel length is short or long.

You should already know the consonant classes (or at least know most of them); item 2 is determined by the individual components of the syllable (or word).

Live and Dead Syllables

There are 2 rules to determine whether a syllable is live or dead:

- If a syllable <u>ends with a short vowel</u>, or it <u>ends with a stop final</u> consonant, it is a **dead syllable**.

- If a syllable <u>ends with a long vowel</u> or it <u>ends with a sonorant final</u> consonant then it is a **live syllable**.

For example:

- ละ – this word ends with short vowel (สระ -ะ [3]) therefore it is a dead syllable.

- ยาก – though it has a long vowel (สระ -า) it ends with a stop final consonant (/**k**/ - remember as a final consonant, ก makes the unaspirated /**k**/ sound) and is therefore a dead syllable.

Live or Dead?

It's all about the end:
*- short/stop = **dead***
*- long/sonorant = **live***

- ยา – ends with a long vowel (สระ -า) and is therefore a live syllable.

- ยาว – ends with a sonorant final consonant (/**o**/) and is a live syllable.

So you can see, it is easy to work out. Just remember, *it's all about the end:* **dead-end,** or **live-end**.

Calculating the Tone

Once we know the consonant class (High, Middle or Low) and the syllable type (Live or Dead), we can use Table 15 to calculate the tone:

Table 15. **Calculating Tone (the hard way)**

Syllable Type	Consonant Class		
	Low Class	**Middle Class**	**High Class**
Dead Syllable	Short Vowel: *high tone (/)*	low tone (\)	low tone (\)
	Long Vowel: *falling tone (^)*		
Live Syllable	mid tone	mid tone	rising tone (v)

The table is straightforward but just to clarify how we calculate Low Class consonants with a dead syllable: if the vowel used is short, e.g. ละ, then the

---

3. The word สระ (sà-rà) means vowel and is always used when referring to vowels.

tone will be *high tone* (lá); whereas, if the vowel is long, e.g. ยาก, then the tone will be *falling tone* (yâak).

With transliterated Thai we use diacritics to specify tone; but, from the last two sections you can see that with written Thai syllable and word tone is encompassed within the writing system itself.

Thinking back to our restaurant example, even though *Sawasdee* (สวัสดี) is not actually written in translitered text (it's a restaurant name), we also should remember that there is no 's' final sound in the Thai language (refer to Table 11 and Table 12): so, with this in mind the correct pronunciation is actually sà-wàt-dii (second syllable is a dead syllable and is therefore low tone).

Does it make a real difference?

In this example, of course not, there's very little harm done and you will be understood from the context; but, it just won't sound exactly right. Don't worry though, Thai people are so pleased when foreigners try and learn their language that they'll help you get it right. The thing is, if you're going to learn it, then why not get it right from the outset?

Remembering Tone Rules

As you've just seen (and can probably imagine), remembering the tone rules can be quite time consuming if no tone mark is present as it has to be done with <u>every single syllable or word</u>. The good news is that we have a much easier way for you.

Russ created these acronyms to aid remember the tone rules:

- **H**arry **D**rinks **L**ager (**H**igh [class consonant] + **D**ead [syllable] = **L**ow [tone]) **HDL**

- **H**arry **L**ikes **R**ed Stripe (**H**igh + **L**ive = **R**ising) **HLR**

- **M**ike **D**rinks **L**ager (**M**iddle + **D**ead = **L**ow) **MDL**

- Mike Likes Miller (**Middle** + **Live** = **Middle**) **MLM**

- Lesley Drinks SHandy (**Low** + **Dead** + **Short** [vowel] = **High**) **LDSH**

- Lesley Drinks Lager Fast (**Low** + **Dead** + **Long** [vowel] = **Falling**) **LDLF**

- Lesley Likes Miller (**Low** + **Live** = **Middle**) **LLM**

For example:

- HDL
- HLR
- MDL
- MLM
- LDSH
- LDLF
- LLM

- สอด - **High** Class consonant + **Dead** syllable = *low tone* (**HDL**)

- ขวา - **High** Class consonant + **Live** syllable = *rising tone* (**HLR**)

- ปิด - **Middle** Class consonant + **Dead** syllable = *low tone* (**MDL**)

- ไป - **Middle** Class consonant + **Live** syllable = *mid tone* (**MLM**)

- รับ - **Low** Class consonant + **Dead** syllable and **SH**ort vowel = *high tone* (**LDSH**)

- มาก - **Low** Class consonant + **Dead** syllable and **Long** vowel = *falling tone* (**LDLF**)

- ฟัง - **Low** Class consonant + **Live** syllable = *mid tone* (**LLM**)

Learning these acronyms will really help you master calculating tone; and, after a bit of practice, you should be able to do it very quickly. We use this 'formula' throughout the book so it will be drilled into you in no time at all.

Multi-Role Consonants

Thai has two consonants that have multiple roles: **High Class** ห (*humps*) and **Middle Class** อ (*awful (weather)*); and these multiple roles affect pronunciation and syllable/word tone.

As we've already covered, these 2 consonants can be used as voiced consonants, where they make the /**h**/ and /**aw**/ sounds respectively; but, they can also be used as either silent consonants, or as vowel placement consonants: where they make no sound at all (in either case). However, it must be added that though อ is frequently seen as a vowel placement consonant, ห never is. It may sound confusing, but we will explain what these latter two terms actually mean next.

Silent Consonants

What is a silent consonant?

A silent consonant is one that is not spoken and is used to change the tone of a syllable or a word (we write syllable or word, as a word can consist of one or more syllables). In Thai, there are 2 types of silent consonant:

- Preceding consonants (ห and อ)

- Vowel placement consonants (อ)

Also, there is a symbol in Thai which, though it is not a silent consonant itself, makes the consonant it is written above, silent. This symbol is called the Gaa-ran (-่), refer to page 142.

Preceding Consonants

Preceding consonants are always found at the beginning of a syllable (or word). They have a number of rules associated with them, and though they are a bit more complex, and we want to keep it simple at this stage, once you're comfortable with the language, reading, etc., you can then brush up on these in Appendix E - Preceding Consonants, and Appendix F - Silent อ.

At this stage, it's far easier for us to remember them collectively as silent consonants; but, why do we need them? Well, the answer is to do with tone.

Thai is a tonal language and, as we have already shown, has certain rules attached to it. If you study the tone marks and tone rules of the language, you will see that though Middle Class or High Classconsonants can produce a *low tone* sound (via the syllable or word having a dead syllable or by using Mái èek) it is impossible for a syllable or word beginning with a Low Class consonant to make a *low tone* sound.

To elaborate, a **Low Class** consonant with a **live syllable** will give *mid tone*. A **Low Class** consonant with a **dead syllable** will produce either a *high tone* if it has a short vowel, or a *falling tone* if it has a long vowel. Though *rising tone* with a Low Class consonant can be obtained through the use of the tone mark **Mái jàt-dtà-waa** (-̇), this is rarely seen.

Nevertheless, there is still no method of actually producing a *low tone* sylla-ble or word with a Low Class initial consonant. The only way this can actually happen is to 'transform' the Low Class syllable or word into a High Class or a Middle Class syllable - this is one of the main roles of the silent consonant.

We'll illustrate this in the following examples:

Example 1 - มาด

For example 1, we have the word มาด, which has **Low Class** ม as its initial consonant (/**m**/ as in *map*); and, even though it has a long vowel (สิระ -า),

which makes the long /**aa**/ as in *palm* sound, ด is a stop final consonant, which makes it a **dead syllable** (Middle Class *d*amsel *t*ower gives us a /**d**/ sonorant sound as an initial consonant, but a /**t**/ final stop sound as a termi-nal consonant - refer to page 25 if you need clarification).

Stop Final Sounds
There are 3:
*/**k**/, /**p**/, and /**t**/*

(ก, บ, and ด)

Putting these together we have:

$$/m/ + /aa/ + /t/ = /maat/$$

Once we've worked out the sound each syllable or word makes, we must now calculate tone.

Tone Rules

As no tone mark is present, we must calculate tone. To do this, we need to know the consonant class: **High**, **Middle**, or **Low**; the type of syllable: **live** or **dead**; and, if the consonant class is low tone and the syllable is **dead**, whether the vowel is long or short. This may seem like a huge amount to learn, but it isn't if you learn the acronyms (page 27).

The consonant is **Low Class** (ม), the syllable is a **dead** syllable as it has a stop final consonant sound /t/ (from consonant ด), and the vowel is a **long** vowel (สระ -า). So, we have **Low**, **Dead**, **Long**. Which acronym begins **LDL...**? It's **LDLF**: 'Lesley Drinks Lager Fast'. The acronym tells us it's **F**, *falling tone.*

In this book, we write this tone '*calculation*' in full as follows:

Low Class consonant + **D**ead syllable and **L**ong vowel = *falling tone* (**LDLF**)

Now we've worked out the tone, we can write the *falling tone* transliterated tone mark:

มาด = mâat (appearance or manner)

Preceding Written ห

Remember that we're talking about Silent Consonants, so if we add **High Class** ห as a preceding consonant, the word then becomes หมาด. We write that it's silent in front of the calculation (it *precedes* it):

/silent/ + /m/ + /aa/ + /t/ = /<u>maat</u>/

As the initial consonant sound is silent, we change the initial sound after the equals sign to reflect the class change to a High Class initial consonant (**Note**: the consonant doesn't actually change class, it's just the way we write it for clarity). Naturally you can't see the colour change with black text, so we underline the initial consonant for you.

Next, we have to calculate the tone. We now have a **High Class** initial consonant and a **D**ead syllable; what acronym begins with HD?

It's '**H**arry **D**rinks **L**ager' - **HDL**. This means the tone is *low tone*. We write this as follows:

High Class consonant + **D**ead syllable = *low tone* (**HDL**)

We can now apply the transliteration tone sign:

หมาด = màat (*almost dry*)

As the example shows, using a silent consonant creates a different tone for the word and, as Thai is a tonal language, a totally new word.

We'll now look at a second example using the other consonant, Middle Class อ อ่าง.

Note: there is also a **_Preceding Unwritten ห_** in Thai, and this will be explained in full as we proceed through the book.

Example 2 - ยาก

Stop Final Sounds
There are 3:
/k/, /p/, and /t/

(ก, บ, and ด)

ยาก has **Low Class** ย as the initial consonant (/y/ as in **y**eti ice) and **Middle Class** ก as the final consonant (/k/ as in galahad **k**night). /k/ is a stop sound (page 25), so this makes the syllable a **dead syllable**. As we have a **Low Class** consonant and a **dead** syllable we also need to know the length of the vowel: /aa/ (as in p**a**lm) is a **long** vowel. This gives us:

/y/ + /aa/ + /k/ = /yaak/

Next we calculate tone.

Tone Rules

What acronym begins with **LDL** (Low Class, Dead syllable, Long vowel)? It's **LDLF** again: 'Lesley Drinks Lager Fast' – *falling tone*.

***Remembering
Tone Rules***

- HDL
- HLR
- MDL
- MLM
- LDSH
- LDLF
- LLM

Low Class consonant + **D**ead syllable and **L**ong vowel = *falling tone* (**LDLF**)

ยาก = yâak (*hard, difficult*)

Preceding อ

If we now place **Middle Class** อ as the preceding consonant to form the

word อยาก, we write **/silent/** in the same manner and get:

/silent/ + /y/ + /aa/ + /k/ = /y̱aak/

Next we calculate tone.

Tone Rules

We have **Middle Class** and **D**ead syllable (**MD**), what acronym begins **MD**? It's '**M**ike **D**rinks **L**ager (**MDL**) and therefore the tone is *low tone*:

Middle Class consonant + **D**ead syllable = *low tone* (**MDL**)

อยาก = yàak (*would like*)

Again, the tone has changed and a new word is created.

Note: *though preceding consonant ห หีบ is used with many words in Thai, preceding consonant อ อ่าง is only used with 4 words (refer to Appendix F - Silent อ).*

Vowel Placement Consonants

To understand vowel placement consonants, consider the English personal pronoun 'I', or the indefinite article 'a'. We can call these vowels free-standing as they don't need a consonant to assist them.

Rule 2

Every vowel must have a consonant.

This is different to Thai where every vowel has to be written, or associated 'with' a consonant. In the next section, we cover the 8 rules in detail, but this rule is number 2; and, regardless of where the vowel is written: in front, above, behind, or below, it has to be written with a consonant. Even unwritten vowels either come between two consonants in the same syllable, or two consonants in different syllables (we cover this soon, on page 44); <u>vowels cannot stand alone</u>.

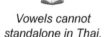

Vowels cannot standalone in Thai.

This produces the situation where, if all we want to reproduce is the vowel sound, we need to have some way of 'silencing' the consonant [sound]. This is the role of the vowel placement consonant.

Let us illustrate this with an example:

Example – Vowel Placement

For example, we have the word อีก. This word is pronounced /**iik**/.

It is comprised of **Middle Class** อ (/ɔɔ/ as in *awful (weather)*), the long vowel which makes the /ii/ as in *steeple* sound, and **Middle Class** ก as the final consonant (/**k**/ as in *galahad knight*).

However, as specified in the previous section, อ cannot be a preceding consonant here as there are only 4 words in the Thai language to which it acts in this capacity. Therefore, the only role which allows us to produce just the vowel sound is when อ it is acting as a vowel placement consonant.

For all intents and purposes they are the same, so in our system we write a vowel placement consonant in the same way as we write /**silent**/ consonants:

$$/\textbf{silent}/ + /ii/ + /k/ = /\underline{ii}k/$$

As always, when there is no tone mark, we must calculate tone.

Remembering Tone Rules

- HDL
- HLR
- MDL
- MLM
- LDSH
- LDLF
- LLM

Our [vowel placement] consonant is **M**iddle Class, the syllable is **D**ead, what acronym do we need?

'**M**ike **D**rinks **L**ager (**MDL**)' - the tone is *low tone.* We write it as:

Middle Class consonant + **D**ead syllable = *low tone* (**MDL**)

อีก = iik (*again*)

Once you're comfortable with what you've just learnt you can move onto reading Thai with a better understanding of how it all fits together. On the next pages are some short exercises to reinforce what you've just been through. After completing them, we will look at some very simple rules which are essential in helping you to learn to read.

Notes

Exercise 1

Exercise 1a

*Answers begin on
page 341*

Each of the following has a tone mark, calculate the tone:

1. ไก่   4. ไพ่   7. ไล่

2. ได้   5. เหล่า   8. โต๊ะ

3. ไส้   6. เว้น   9. ไข่

1. <u>Middle</u> Class consonant + Mái èek (-่) = <u>*low*</u> tone

2. _____ Class consonant + Mái -๋ = _____ tone

3. _____ Class consonant + Mái -๋ = _____ tone

4. _____ Class consonant + Mái -่ = _____ tone

5. _____ Class consonant + Mái -่ = _____ tone

6. _____ Class consonant + Mái -๋ = _____ tone

7. _____ Class consonant + Mái -่ = _____ tone

8. _____ Class consonant + Mái -๊ = _____ tone

9. _____ Class consonant + Mái -่ = _____ tone

Exercise 1b

- If a syllable ends with a _____ vowel, or it ends with a _____ final consonant, it is a dead syllable.

- If a syllable ends with a _____ vowel, or it ends with a _____ final consonant, it is a _____ syllable.

Exercise 1c

Work out the tone of the following words:

1. ไกล	4. ลม	7. หมู
2. สิบ	5. นก	8. จะ
3. ไป	6. พูด	

We've done the first one for you (don't forget the vowel length is also important for **Low Class dead** syllables):

Remembering Tone Rules
- HDL
- HLR
- MDL
- MLM
- LDSH
- LDLF
- LLM

1. ไกล = **Middle** Class (ก) + **Live** syllable = *mid* tone (**MLM**)

2.

3.

4.

5.

6.

7.

8.

The Rules for Reading Thai

In this section, we cover the rules for reading Thai. In our previous material we referred to 6 main rules for reading Thai and also 2 unwritten tone rules; but, as they're so important, we think it makes more sense to just talk about 8 rules and that way you know exactly which rule we're referring to.

These rules are fundamental in learning to read Thai effectively, so the sooner you learn them the easier you will be able to follow us and the better off you will be.

The good thing is they're not difficult to learn; but, as they help ensure that everything we talk about from here makes sense, they are essential to know. We will repeat them again and again, but try and learn them before you proceed further.

The Rules

1. Every syllable starts with a consonant. Though the first character written in a syllable will not always be a consonant **the consonant is always pronounced first**.

2. A written vowel is always associated with a consonant. In English, we have 'free-standing' vowels such as 'I' and 'A', but **in Thai, every vowel must have a consonant**.

3. **A vowel is always written in the same place in relation to a conso-nant**, its position does not change. Some vowels are written before, some below, some above and some after the consonant; but they are always written in the same position.

4. สระ ไ-, ใ-, -ะ and -ำ are **never** followed by a final consonant [4].

5. สระ -ำ and -ะ **always** mark the end of a syllable.

6. สระ -ี is **always** followed by a final consonant.

With the exception of rule 1, which is about consonants, the oth-ers are all about vowels. It is this crucial knowledge that helps us, as beginners, to identify words and syllables in Thai sentences; and, why understanding these rules is key to learning to read with Quest: Quick, Easy, Simple Thai.

Look for the vowels!

Now we'll look at the 2 unwritten vowel rules.

Unwritten Vowel Rules

It is the unwritten vowel rules which trip the beginner up, so learn, repeat, and remember them:

7. Unwritten /o/ (สระ โ-) occurs between 2 consonants in the **same sylla-ble**.

8. Unwritten /a/ (สระ -ะ) occurs between 2 consonants in **different sylla-bles**.

It's vital that you understand these unwritten vowel rules so we'll look at 2 examples to illustrate how they are used.

---

4. Remember, สระ (sà-rà) means vowel.

Examples

Example 1 – ผม

Remember, **always look for the vowels**.

In our first example, we can't see any written vowels. All we have are 2 consonants: one is **High Class** ผ and the other is **Low Class** ม. They make the /**p**/ as in *p*rofits, and the /**m**/ as in *m*ap sounds, respectively.

We've already stated that every syllable or word must have a consonant and a vowel; and, as we cannot see a written vowel here it must be unwritten.

The unwritten vowel rule to apply depends on whether the 2 consonants which span the unwritten vowel are in the same or in different syllables. Which is it?

Rule 7

*Unwritten /o/ occurs between 2 consonants in the **same syllable**.*

This is obviously a 1-syllable word – unless a consonant cluster was present, it would require at least 1 more consonant for there to be 2 syllables: a Thai syllable or word can have just 1 consonant and vowel – and as the 2 consonants have to be in the same syllable, rule 7 states:

'Unwritten /**o**/ (สระ โ-) occurs between 2 consonants
in the **same syllable**.'

We then place unwritten /**o**/ between the consonants:

/**p**/ + /**o**/ + /**m**/ = /**pom**/

The next thing we must do with **every syllable or word**, is work out its tone.

- HDL
- HLR
- MDL
- MLM
- LDSH
- LDLF
- LLM

Tone Rules

We have a **H**igh Class consonant and a **L**ive syllable (/**m**/ sonorant sound). What acronym begins with **HL**?

It's '**H**arry **L**ikes **R**ed Stripe (**HLR**)' - this word is *Rising tone*.

Now we know the tone, we can place the diacritic that indicates rising tone.

ผม = pŏm (it is the male first person personal pronoun, 'I', or 'me')

Now, we'll look at a slightly more complex example.

Example 2 - How Complex is Fruit?

The Thai word for fruit is ผลไม้.

Again, this is quite a unique and fairly complex example, but please bear with us as it illustrates 3 important points:

1. It helps understand unwritten vowels.

2. It gives an insight into some of the intricacies and difficulties with learning the Thai language.

3. It highlights the importance of having a good English-Thai dictionary in your possession (if you haven't got one already, please remedy that).

At first glance, ผลไม้ looks like it has two syllables: ผล-ไม้; but, as a beginner, how do we even know this small amount?

The First Syllable

We know ผล is the first syllable because we see the vowel ไ- immediately after the ล (ผล**ไม้**). If you remember back to Table 7 on page 22, this particular vowel is **always written before** an initial consonant [in a syllable or word]; therefore, we know that ม has to be the initial consonant for this vowel and also the initial consonant of the 2nd syllable (ผล**ไม้**); and, as it's the initial consonant of the next syllable, then ล **has to be** the final consonant of the previous one (it can't be anything else - ผล**ไม้**).

The vowel สระ ไ- (and its counterpart สระ ใ-) <u>always</u> gives us a clear indication of a syllable or word break.

The first consonant of the first syllable is obviously ผ. Remembering this consonant is a **High Class** consonant which makes the /**p**/ sound (remember *p*rofits). The second consonant in the first syllable (ล) is a **Low Class** consonant which makes the /**l**/ sound when it is an initial consonant, and the /**n**/ sound when it is in the final position in a syllable or word (remember *l*arge *n*ugget); therefore, as it is in the final consonant position in this syllable, it makes the /**n**/ sound. This gives us:

/**p**/ + /**n**/

Rule 7

*Unwritten /o/ occurs between 2 consonants in the **same syllable**.*

As the consonants are in the same syllable and there is no written vowel, rule 7 applies here; and therefore, exactly as in the previous example, the unwritten vowel has to be /**o**/. So, this first syllable is:

/**p**/ + /**o**/ + /**n**/ = /**pon**/

Tone Rules

As mentioned, in Thai, every syllable and word has one of 5 tones. If there is no tone mark present, then <u>you must always</u> calculate tone. With this part of the word we have the same construction as before (**H**arry **L**ikes **R**ed Stripe - go back and review the previous example if you're unsure of this):

- HDL
- HLR
- MDL
- MLM
- LDSH
- LDLF
- LLM

High Class consonant + **L**ive syllable = *rising tone* (**HLR**)

Therefore, this part of the word is:

pǒn

The Second Syllable

The second syllable is ไม้

Rule 4

Sà-rà ไ-, ใ-, -ะ *and* ◌ำ *are **never** followed by a final consonant.*

Rule 4 states that ไ- is never followed by a **final** consonant (Table 7 tells us this consonant is always written before an initial consonant - they're the same thing). Because of this, สระ ไ- (and its counterpart สระ ใ-) always start a new syllable or word.

This particular syllable is comprised of ไ-, which makes the /**ai**/ as in *knight* sound, and is **always written before** the consonant; the **Low Class** consonant ม, which makes the /**m**/ as in *map* sound; plus, tone mark Mái too (◌้). This syllable is written as:

Rule 1

The consonant is always pronounced first.

/**ai**/ + /**m**/

Do you remember rule 1, that **every syllable starts with a consonant**? In order to pronounce this, we swap the vowel and consonant positions so the consonant is pronounced first:

/**m**/ + /**ai**/

Next, we must calculate tone.

Tone

Tone Marks

if a tone mark is present, it overrides all other tone rules.

Remember, if a tone mark is present, this overrides all other tone rules (page 29).

Low Class consonant (ม) + Mái too (◌้) = *high tone*

This syllable is:

ไม้

mái

Putting both syllables together, you would think this is

/pǒn/ + /mái/

However, it isn't a 2-syllable word, it's actually a 3-syllable word which is pro-nounced *pŏn-lá-mái.* There is no way you would actually know this and it helps to illustrate an occasional peculiarity and difficulty with learning new words in Thai.

The Third Syllable

Where did this middle syllable come from?

As I mentioned, this is quite a complex example, but it is a characteristic of a few words in Thai (and only a few words thankfully) that the <u>final consonant</u> of the first syllable, which is ล in this example, becomes the <u>first consonant</u> of the next syllable. Then, as it becomes the first, or initial letter of the next syllable, we must use its *initial consonant sound* to find the new syllable sound. So, for this example, the initial consonant sound is /l/ *as in large nug-get.*

Previously, we mentioned that every syllable has to have a consonant and a vowel; and, as we can't see one written, we have to apply the unwritten vowel rules. So, for our new syllable, which one do we use?

We've already established that /l/ is an initial consonant; and, as an initial consonant, it <u>has to be</u> the initial consonant in its own syllable. Therefore, the unwritten vowel has to be between this consonant and the initial conso-nant in the subsequent syllable, which puts them in **different syllables**; and, therefore rule 8 applies:

*Rule 8
Unwritten /a/
occurs between
2 consonants in
**different sylla-
bles**.*

'Unwritten /**a**/ (สิระ -ะ) occurs between 2 consonants in **different sylla-bles**.'

Tone Rules

As always, we calculate tone (even for a hidden syllable).

- HDL
- HLR
- MDL
- MLM
- LDSH
- LDLF
- LLM

We know it's a **Low** Class consonant; and, with a short vowel we know it's a dead syllable. What acronym does a **Low** Class consonant with a **Dead** syllable and a **SH**ort vowel have? **L**arry **D**rinks **SH**andy...

Low Class + **Dead** syllable and **S**hort vowel = *high tone* (**LDSH**)

We write this example phonetically as:

ผน-ละ-ไม้ = ผลไม้

ผลไม้ = pǒn-lá-mái.

Now, don't get too worried as this is quite an extreme and complex example; but, it helps you to understand that this is a problem when encountering unfamiliar words and why it pays to have a dictionary handy.

Now you see how we apply the acronyms each time, we will discontinue spelling it out in this manner and just jump straight to the calculation.

We've covered the vast majority of the rules now and we do realise there's a lot to take in at first; but, we've included a quick end of section summary to help you. After that, we can then start looking at the simple vowels.

Section Summary

Thai Alphabet

The Thai alphabet consists of:

- 44 consonants (2 of which are obsolete).

- 32 vowels: divided up into simple (20 of) and complex vowels (12 of); and, further sub-divided into short and long.

- We use the Paiboon system where short vowels use a single vowel letter (/**a**/) and long vowels use a double-vowel letter (/**aa**/).

Consonant Classes

Consonant class is a prime factor in determining word and syllable tone and all consonants belong to one of the 3 classes:

- High Class (11 of)

- Middle Class (9 of)

- Low Class (24 of).

Consonant Clusters

- Consonant clusters are where two consonants combine to form a **single spoken consonant** and there is no unwritten vowel between them.

- Vowels and tone marks are always written above or beneath the second consonant in the cluster.

- There are 5 initial consonant cluster sounds:
  /**g**/ (ก); /**k**/ (ข and ค); /**dt**/ (ต); /**bp**/ (ป); and, /**p**/ (ผ and พ).

- The second consonant in a cluster will always be either /**r**/ (ร), /**l**/ (ล), or /**w**/ (ว).

Multi-role Consonants

In addition to their normal spoken consonant role, two consonants have additional roles:

1. High Class ห (h*umps*) and Middle Class อ (aw*ful (weather)*) - Preceding consonants.

2. Middle Class อ (aw*ful (weather)*) - Vowel placement consonant.

Sonorant and Stop Sounds

There are 5 sonorant sounds and 3 stop sounds.

- Sonorant: /**ng**/ (ง), /**n**/ (น), /**m**/ (ม), /**i**/ (ย), /**o**/ (ว)

- Stop: /**k**/ (ก), /**t**/ (ด), and /**p**/ (บ).

These sounds are used to determine the syllable type.

Live or Dead Syllable:

- Syllable or word ends in a **short vowel** or **stop** sound = **dead syllable**
- Syllable or word ends in a **long vowel** or **sonorant** sound = **live syllable**

Tone

- Thai has 5 tones: *high*, *falling*, *middle*, *rising*, and *low*.
- Every syllable and word has to have one of these tones.
- If a tone mark is not present, you must calculate the tone of every single syllable and word.

Tone Rules:

- Harry Drinks Lager (High [class consonant] + Dead [syllable] = Low [tone]) **HDL**

- Harry Likes Red Stripe (High + Live = Rising) **HLR**

- Mike Drinks Lager (Middle + Dead = Low) **MDL**

- Mike Likes Miller (Middle + Live = Middle) **MLM**

- Lesley Drinks SHandy (Low + Dead + Short [vowel] = High) **LDSH**

- Lesley Drinks Lager Fast (Low + Dead + Long [vowel] = Falling) **LDLF**

- Lesley Likes Miller (Low + Live = Middle) **LLM**

Rules for Reading Thai

1. Every syllable starts with a consonant.

2. A written vowel is always associated with a consonant.

3. A vowel is always written in the same place.

4. สระ ไ-, ใ-, -ะ and -ำ are **never** followed by a final consonant.

5. สระ-ำ and -ะ **always** mark the end of a syllable.

6. สระ ◌ั is always followed by a final consonant.

7. Unwritten /o/ (สระ โ-) occurs between 2 **same** syllable consonants.

8. Unwritten /a/ (สระ -ะ) occurs between 2 **different** syllable consonants.

Simple Vowels

Unwritten Vowels

Identifying where syllables and words start and end is, for the most part, dependent on the vowels; and, as beginners starting to learn to read Thai, this is what we have to look for.

As the 'fruit' example (ผลไม้) showed, you need to be aware that even with this knowledge, sometimes you will need to resort to a good old-fashioned dictionary or other resource to help you.

What we are going to teach you here could be considered a fairly slow method of learning to read Thai; however, it is logical, it is comprehensive, it is sound, and it will teach you how to read Thai. Besides, would you prefer a rapid method that skims over everything, or would you prefer a step-by-step, detailed, and methodical explanation that WILL get you where you want to be?

The simplified process we adopt when looking at any new text (word or sentence, but we'll start with just words for the first part of the book) is this:

1. Find the written vowel(s).

2. Apply rules 2 - 6 and the chances are you now know where a syllable/word starts and ends (Rule 1: consonants are always pronounced first shouldn't be too difficult to remember).

3. Work out if the word is single or multi-syllabic.

We appreciate that this is very much a 'bottom-up' approach to learning, but you have to remember that at this stage, until we can understand some words and work out what sentences (or at least part of them) say, we have no context clues to help us guess or work out the rest.

Naturally, once your reading vocabulary expands, you can then apply the knowledge and experience you already possess to the subject in hand; but, until then, we'll take it step-by-step.

We also recognise that there may be some people out there who have a cunning knack for languages and to them this method may seem strange and slow; but, the think-aloud strategy is an effective teaching method and you following along and taking a firm grasp of the thought process will set you up for where you want to be.

If you recall the section on the Rules for Reading Thai, there are two unwritten vowel rules:

> 7. Unwritten /o/ (สระ โ-) occurs between 2 consonants in the **same syllable**.

> 8. Unwritten /a/ (สระ -ะ) occurs between 2 consonants in **different syllables**.

Unwritten vowels are one of the main contributors to difficulties for learners, so it's important that you fully understand the rules. Let's look at our first example.

Example 1 - บน

We have a word, บน.

This is a common word, and consists of a **Middle Class** initial consonant (/b/ as in *bald patch)*, and a **Low Class** final consonant (/n/ as in *navigating*). Though we have the steps we've just outlined, as we can't see any written vowels then the word has to be a single syllable word, and we've covered the remaining steps in one go. Writing this out, we have:

$$/b/ + /n/$$

As you can see, there is no vowel in this word; but, now we know that <u>every syllable or word must have a consonant and a vowel</u> so there has to be one in there somewhere.

Rule 7

*Unwritten /o/ occurs between 2 consonants in the **same syllable**.*

As it is a single syllable word, the consonants **must be** in the same syllable. We can see that there is no written vowel so the vowel must be unwritten; and, as the consonants are in the same syllable, **rule 7** applies. This word is:

$$/b/ + /o/ + /n/ = /bon/$$

Tone Rules

- HDL
- HLR
- MDL
- MLM
- LDSH
- LDLF
- LLM

As there is no tone mark, we have to calculate the syllable tone (remember, there are <u>no exceptions</u> to this, it must be done every time).

Middle Class consonant (บ) + **L**ive syllable = *mid tone* (**MLM**)

บน = bon (it's a preposition and means *on.)*

We will now look at a slightly harder example.

Example 2 - กรุณา

กรุณา has 3-syllables and is a commonly seen word on signs in commercial buildings and public places.

We will now follows steps 1 & 2 (as we've already said it's multi-syllabic), let us first identify the vowels we can see:

1. We can see a vowel underneath the second consonant (ร), and one

    vowel after the third consonant (ณ).

Rule 2

Every vowel must have a consonant.

2. Rule 2 states a vowel always has to be associated with a consonant:

    a. The first vowel (◌ุ) is <u>always</u> written underneath the first consonant in a syllable or word[5].

    b. The second vowel (-า) is <u>always</u> written after a consonant.

Considering where the first vowel is written, the first 2 consonants could make up a consonant cluster (refer to Table 4 for a complete list of conso-nant clusters): กรุ-ณา

---

5. With the exception of consonant clusters (refer to page 16)

However, after checking our dictionary, we see this is a 3-syllable word and, for that very reason, there isn't a cluster here. Of course, as we couldn't possibly know this we would have to reach for our dictionary or ask a knowledgeable friend.

The 3 syllables in this word are:

ก-รุ-ณา

Having established the written vowels and the syllables (we know it's 3-syllables), we would then work through steps 2-6.

We see that the first syllable doesn't have a written vowel; yet, we now know that every syllable **must have** a vowel, so it must be unwritten.

Which vowel is it, /**o**/ or /**a**/?

To be the former, the consonants have to be in the **same syllable**; but, we already know the next consonant belongs to the second syllable and not to the first (there is a vowel written beneath it which, unless it is part of a consonant cluster, is always written under an **initial** consonant).

Rule 8

*Unwritten /a/ occurs between 2 consonants in **different syllables**.*

Therefore, this unwritten vowel is **between two consonants in different syllables**; and, **Rule 8** states an unwritten vowel between consonants in different syllables must make the /**a**/ sound.

We know that the first consonant (ก) makes the /**g**/ sound (remember *g*alahad *k*night - **Middle Class**) and with the unwritten vowel we have:

/g/ + /a/ + รุณา = /ga/ - รุณา

Moving on to the second syllable:

1. We know that vowels written beneath a consonant are **always** written underneath the initial consonant (with the exception of consonant clusters). Next, the consonant ร is a **Low Class** consonant and it makes the /**r**/ sound when an initial consonant (remember *r*abbit *n*ibbling); and, we

also know the simple vowel (-ฺ) makes the /**u**/ as in *cro**o**k* sound. Together these form the second syllable:

/**r**/ + /**u**/ = /**ru**/

(Remember, rule 1 states the consonant is **always pronounced first**)

2. We now have:

/ga/ - /ru/ - **ณา**

Now for the third syllable.

3. The vowel (-า) is **always** written after an initial consonant (Table 9 on page 23) and it makes the /**aa**/ as in *p**a**lm* sound; we also remember a picture where *N*apoleon is handing out medals to his guard (/**n**/, **Low Class**).

Therefore we have:

/**ga**/ - /**ru**/ - /**n**/ + /**aa**/

/**ga**/-/**ru**/-/**naa**/

Tone Rules

- HDL
- HLR
- MDL
- MLM
- LDSH
- LDLF
- LLM

As there are no tone marks, we need to calculate the tone for each syllable:

- Syllable 1: **M**iddle Class + **D**ead syllable = *low tone* (**MDL**)

- Syllable 2: **L**ow Class + **D**ead syllable and **SH**ort vowel = *high tone* (**LDSH**)

- Syllable 3: **L**ow Class + **L**ive syllable = *mid tone* (**LLM**)

กรุณา = gà-rú-naa (it means *please*)

Quirk with /ɔɔ/

There is an additional modification to unwritten vowel rules 7 & 8, and that is:

Rule 7 - with certain words which end with ร, the unwritten vowel is /ɔɔ/, not /o/, e.g. นคร (ná-kɔɔn - *city*) and จร (jɔɔn - *to roam*), etc.

Rule 8 - when the initial consonant of a syllable is บ the unwritten vowel used is /ɔɔ/, not /a/, e.g พฤหัสบดี (pá-rɰ́-hàt-sà-bɔɔ-dii - *Thursday*)

Exercise 2

Exercise 2a

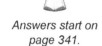

Answers start on page 341.

Work out the unwritten vowels in the following words (there is only 1 unwritten vowel in each of the first 8 words):

1. ขด - /k/ + /o/ + /t/ = /kot/

2. บน - /b/ + / ... / + /n/ = /b ... n/

3. พนัก - /p/ + / ... / + /n/ + /a/ + /k/ = /p ... nak/

4. จด - /j/ + / ... / + / ... / = /j ... ... /

5. จน -

6. ดง -

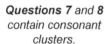

Questions 7 and **8** contain consonant clusters.

7. กลม -

8. พรม -

Exercise 2b

Answers start on page 342.

In this exercise, work out the tone of the words you've just done:

1. ขด - **H**igh Class + **D**ead syllable = *low tone* (**HDL**) = /kòt/

2. บน

- **HDL**
- **HLR**
- **MDL**
- **MLM**
- **LDSH**
- **LDLF**
- **LLM**

3. พนัก

4. จด

5. จน

6. ดง

7. กลม

8. พรม

Simple Vowels

Notes

สระ -ะ & อ้-

In this chapter we look at sà-rà -ะ and อ้- (this second vowel is called Mái Hǎn-aa-ġaat). The word sà-rà (สระ) means *vowel* and both of these vowels make the same short /**a**/ vowel sound. The difference between these two vowels is they are written in **three** different places.

Unlike English vowels, which can make different sounds depending on the actual word, what part of speech it is, or the other consonants in the syllable or word, **the sound of the vowel in Thai remains the same**, even when the consonant changes. That is the beauty and the ease of vowels in Thai, they always make the same sound no matter where they are written or whichever consonant they are written with. This alone makes them easier to learn and to remember.

To clarify, even though the two Thai vowels that make the /**a**/ sound can be written in three different positions, they still only make that single /**a**/ sound. Let us look at the examples (2 vowels written in 3 different positions):

- สระ -ะ – you should know this vowel, it makes the /**a**/ as in *puffin* sound. It is a terminal vowel, which means it's always at the end of a syllable or word (**rule 4**).

- Unwritten /**a**/ – unwritten vowel /**a**/ produces the exact same vowel sound as สระ -ะ, it's just unwritten. Remember rule 8, this is the vowel that appears between two consonants in different syllables.

- อ้- – this shape is a new one but it makes the same vowel sound as สระ -ะ (/**a**/), it is written above the consonant and it is called Mái Hǎn-aa-ġaat (ไม้หันอากาศ - ไม้-หัน-อา-กาศ). It is a medial vowel, which means it is always written between two consonants in the <u>same</u> syllable or word.

สระ -ะ

Rule 4

Sà-rà ไ-, ใ-, -ะ

and -ํา are **never** followed by a final consonant.

สระ -ะ is a short vowel (the long vowel form is สระ -า /**aa**/), and it is always written after a consonant. In addition, it is a terminal vowel (nothing else can come after it in a syllable) and as it always marks either the end of a syllable or word it helps us to identify syllable and word breaks.

สระ -ะ is also used to shorten certain long vowels. We discuss that later in Shortening Vowels on page 129.

Example 1 - ค่ะ

Again, always look for and identify the written vowel. สระ -ะ is always easy to see as it marks the end of a syllable or word and we can see it written after the **Low Class** consonant ค. If you remember, this consonant makes the /**k**/ as in *k*oala sound.

$$/k/ + /a/ = /ka/$$

Tone Mark

There is a tone mark here, so we do not need to calculate the tone; but we still need to match the tone mark with the consonant class to find out what the tone is. So, what tone does Mái èek with a Low Class consonant produce?

Hopefully you can remember a plane flying, and a bomb dropping....*koala, Low Class, and remember the bomb falling... that's it falling tone!*

Low Class + Mái èek (-̀) = *falling tone*

*Remember to keep this vowel short when you pronounce it, it's **kâ** not **kâa**.*

So, the word คะ is written in transliterated text as: kâ

คะ is a very common word used by females and is a particle that is used at the end of a sentence to make it more polite. When you are out and about in Thailand, you will hear it all the time: in conversation, on the television, the radio, etc.

Example 2 - จะ

Another common single syllable word is จะ. Remember the sound the จ makes as an initial consonant (/**j**/ as in **j**abberwocky **t**ail)?

$$/j/ + /a/ = /ja/$$

Tone Rules

- HDL
- HLR
- MDL
- MLM
- LDSH
- LDLF
- LLM

Though it has the same vowel, this time there is no tone mark and we must calculate tone:

Middle Class + **D**ead syllable = *low tone* (**MDL**)

Remember, a dead syllable is one that ends with a short vowel or a stop final consonant. Once we know the word sound and its tone, we can write it as:

jà

จะ = jà (this word means *will* or *shall*)

Example 3 - กะปิ

This is a 2-syllable word.

Knowing what you already do about the vowels and consonants, you should be able to clearly see the two written vowels here; and, in conjunction with what we have gone through already, you can tell straightaway where the syllable break is:

กะ-ปิ

Now we know this, the rest is easy.

We've covered the first consonant before so you should remember that it makes the /g/ sound as an initial consonant (/g/ as in *galahad knight*); and, for the second consonant, you should remember seeing a man stuck at the *bottom [of a] pit* and recall that it makes the diphthong /**bp**/ sound (though we use *bottom pit* to help you remember, this sound is different from the /**b**/ initial consonant sound that ป as in *bald patch* makes).

What vowel is it that is written above the second consonant? Think botox injections and you'll then remember *lip* (สระ $\overset{\frown}{-}$). This then gives us:

/g/ + /a/ + /bp/ + /i/

/ga/ + /bpi/ = /ga-bpi/

Tone Rules

- HDL
- HLR
- MDL
- MLM
- LDSH
- LDLF
- LLM

You will also call to mind that both consonants are **Middle Class**. Calculating the syllable tone, we get:

- Syllable 1: **M**iddle Class + **D**ead syllable = *low tone* (**MDL**)
- Syllable 2: **M**iddle Class + **D**ead syllable = *low tone* (**MDL**)

กะปิ = /gà-bpì/.

This is a common item that you will see in the supermarkets and perhaps get to try - *shrimp paste*.

We hope that now you can see how easy it is to identify the syllable or word break with the สระ -ะ vowel form.

Struggling with Our Clues?

If these clues, picture names, or consonant sounds are either meaningless or confuse you, then we recommend either our book **Memory Aids to Your Great Adventure (MATYGA)** or the web-based **Learn Thai Alphabet application**. Of the 2, the app is more useful as you get access to sounds by native speakers, tests, and so forth; and, it really takes learning the Thai alphabet to the next level (http://www.learnthaialphabet.com).

Unwritten Vowel

Rule 8
Unwritten /a/ occurs between 2 consonants in **different syllables**.

You have already encountered the unwritten vowel /**a**/, it is the unwritten version of สระ -ะ and is the vowel referred to in rule 8.

Next, we'll look at the medial, or what is also referred to as the _reduced_, form of สระ -ะ, Mái Hăn-aa-ġaat (อั-).

Mái Hăn-aa-ġaat

Mái Hăn-aa-ġaat provides us with the third use of the vowel sound /**a**/.

Mái Hăn-aa-ġaat (ไม้หันอากาศ - ไม้-หัน-อา-กาศ) is a medial vowel: it is always written between two consonants in the same syllable (as opposed to unwritten /a/ which is between 2 consonants in different syllables).

We write Mái Hăn-aa-ġaat as อั-. Here, อ indicates the initial consonant position and the dash (-) shows the final consonant position.

Why do we need ไม้หันอากาศ?

We have already seen that the vowel สระ -ะ makes the /a/ sound when it is in the terminal position; and, we saw the same vowel when it is unwritten; but, neither of these can provide us with an /a/ sound **between** two consonants in the **same** syllable. This is where Mái Hăn-aa-ġaat (อั-) comes in. Let's look at an example:

สวัสดี

สวัสดี is a very common word, which we used as an example before, and you first see it in the splash screen when you start the *Learn Thai Alphabet application*. As always, we identify the vowels first.

We have Mái Hăn-aa-ġaat (อั-) between the second and third consonants (-วัส-), and we have สระ ◌ี (-ดี) above the final consonant.

We know สระ ◌ี is written above the first consonant in any syllable (with the exception of consonant clusters of course); and, according to Table 4 on page 17, as ส and ด never form consonant clusters, we know ด has to be the initial consonant of the end syllable:

สวัส-ดี

The rules tell us that Mái Hăn-aa-ġaat (อั-) is written between 2 consonants so we can easily see the next syllable but we have to consider the first two consonants (สว-), do they form a consonant cluster?

We look at Table 3 on page 16 and see ส is never used in consonant clusters, so the answer is no there is no cluster here. Therefore, as they don't form a consonant cluster and there is no written vowel between them, then they must be in different syllables.

Our 3-syllable word is:

ส-วัส-ดี

First syllable

Can you remember the first consonant and the sound it makes?

ส makes the /**s**/ sound as an initial consonant (/**s**/ as in *squirrel tail*) and is a **High Class** consonant.

We know that every consonant has to have a vowel and as there is no written vowel, it **must be unwritten**. We have already worked out that ส and ว are in different syllables and according to rule 8 the vowel sound has to be /**a**/.

/**s**/ + /**a**/ + วัส-ดี

/**sa**/ + วัส-ดี

Second syllable

For our second syllable, the first consonant ว makes the /**w**/ as in *w*ave *o*ver sound as an initial consonant and is a **Low Class** consonant.

Next, we have Mái Hăn-aa-ġaat, which makes the /**a**/ sound and the last consonant in this syllable is ส.

As we discussed in our introductory example, we see ส in both the initial and the terminal position in this word; and, when it's a terminal (or final) consonant it makes the /**t**/ as in *s*quirrel *t*ail sound. We now have:

$$\text{/sà/ + /w/ + /a/ + /t/ + ดี}$$

$$\text{/sà/ + /wat/ + ดี}$$

Third syllable

In the last syllable, we quickly recall that when ด is an initial consonant it makes the /d/ as in **d**amsel [in a] **t**ower sound. We also recall the vowel as making the /ii/ as in st**ee**ple sound (remembering that a double-letter is a long vowel with the Paiboon system).

This now gives us:

$$\text{/sà/ + /silent/* + /wat/ + /d/ + /ii/}$$

$$\text{/sà/ + /wat/ + /dii/ = /sa-wat-dii/}$$

* see below.

Tone Rules

We know that every syllable or word has to have one of the five tones and that in the absence of tone marks, we must calculate tone.

In this example, High Class unwritten ห is added as a preceding consonant to the second syllable; and, as Appendix E - Preceding Consonants on page 335 states, it changes the class of that syllable:

- HDL
- HLR
- MDL
- MLM
- LDSH
- LDLF
- LLM

- Syllable 1: **H**igh Class + **D**ead syllable = *low tone* (**HDL**)
- Syllable 2: **H**igh Class + **D**ead syllable = *low tone* (**HDL**)
- Syllable 3: **M**iddle Class + **L**ive syllable = *mid tone* (**MLM**)

สวัสดี = sà-wàt-dii (*hello, hi, good morning, good afternoon,* and *goodbye*).

After this chapter, we hope you can see that though this is perhaps long-winded for you to work through, you can see the think-aloud thought process behind analysing and reading Thai script.

We fully understand that doing it this way is not for everyone; but, as mentioned in the Introduction, this is how I myself learnt to break-down sentences in Thai.

The method we use here is step-by-step and, once you start reading, this all becomes second nature and words do jump out of the page at you. Of course, it takes practice to get to that stage and there's no other place to start than at the beginning.

Take it from me, and I have read many books on learning Thai, I haven't seen any 'How to Read Thai' books that actually tell you the detailed thought process that we have here. I have spoken to Thai teachers and it has to be said, most resort to children's books to teach foreigners and teach in the same manner as teaching a child.

The problem is, you have to understand that learning a first language (L1) as a child is vastly different to learning a second language (L2) as an adult. Adults just don't soak up information in the same way a child does. It's part of our genetic make-up. So, though some articles, books, teachers and language schools will say you need to teach adults a new language in the same way as you would a child, it doesn't quite work like that.

Can I prove this to you?

If you haven't done so already, go to your web-browser and search on your favourite Internet search engine for books about learning Thai – there will be dozens. Next, search for books on how to read Thai – I guarantee these will be few and far between. If what the articles, books, teachers, and schools say is true, your search results would be flooded with book options wouldn't it?

Don't get me wrong, reading Thai is the easy part, comprehension and translation is another matter; but, we will do our best to get you to the stage where you are fully equipped to take it to the next level with your own independent study.

Thanks,

Russ

Exercise 3

Exercise 3a

Answers start on page 343

Match the words to their meaning:

1.	กะปิ	on (preposition)	a.
2.	บน	will, shall	b.
3.	สวัสดี	hello	c.
4.	ค่ะ	please	d.
5.	กรุณา	shrimp paste	e.
6.	จะ	polite particle used by females	f.
7.	สวัสดี	goodbye	g.

Exercise 3b

Identify the syllables in these words (either draw a vertical line, underline them, or even write them out - you can do so below).

1. กะว่า   4. ระบบ

2. ประเทศ   5. ทะเล

3. กระดาน   6. สะบัด

If you want to write them out, do so here:

1.

2.

3.

4.

5.

6.

Exercise 3c

Work out the tone of the following words:

1. หัก   4. ฟัน   7. กระ

2. มด   5. ดัง   8. สัก

3. บท   6. สง   9. ช่ำ

1. หัก = High Class + _____ Syllable = _____ tone (_____)

- HDL
- HLR
- MDL
- MLM
- LDSH
- LDLF
- LLM

2.

3.

4.

5.

6.

7.

8.

9.

สระ ำ

The next vowel we're going to look at is สระ ำ (sà-rà /**am**/). This is the first vowel we come to in Table 5 on page 19.

สระ ำ is a long vowel and the good news is that syllables containing this vowel are **always** live syllables for tone rule purposes.

We write the sound this vowel makes as /**am**/, the sound you make when you pronounce it is similar to that of the **um** in *um*brella.

How is it used?

- สระ ำ is **always** written **after** a consonant.

- สระ ำ **always** marks the end of a syllable.

/consonant sound/ + /am/

Also, as สระ ำ always marks the end of a syllable, the consonant before it **must be** an initial consonant.

With these points in mind, and continuing logically, if we know the word to be a single syllable word then the next character/consonant has to be the start of a new word; however, if we know the word to be more than one syllable then the next character has to be the start of the next syllable.

Do we know, or can we work out, the next syllable? If the answer is yes, continue on; if the answer is no, then it's either reach for the dictionary, ask someone, or write it down to refer to later.

I know this may sound difficult to some, particularly lengthy or even obvious to others, but for those just starting out learning, it helps to have it all explained in logical, easy steps otherwise it may leave questions unanswered.

Once you know these basic rules and can identify syllable and word ends, you're now on your way to breaking a sentence down into its component parts.

For example, here are three words that use this particular vowel:

- ทำ
- กำลัง
- ประจำปี

You should be able to identify all the vowels used here.

Example 1 - ทำ

With the rules we've just mentioned, it is obvious that ทำ is a single syllable word.

This particular initial consonant is **Low Class**, and it makes the /t/ as in *typist* sound (regardless of where in a syllable/word it is located):

$$/t/ + /am/ = /tam/$$

Tone Rules

There is no tone mark present and we must calculate tone:

Low Class + Live syllable = *mid tone* (**LLM**)

ทำ = tam (it means *to do, to make*)

Example 2 - กำลัง

The second example is กำลัง

We've already said that สระ -ำ marks the end of a syllable, so you can easily identify the end of the first syllable and the beginning of the second. We covered the vowel used in the second syllable in the previous chapter.

The initial consonant of the first syllable is /**g**/ as in *galahad knight*, therefore the first syllable is:

/**g**/ + /**am**/ = /**gam**/

The second syllable begins with **Low Class** ล (/**l**/ *as in large nugget)*, then medial Mái Hăn-aa-ġaat (/**a**/) as the written, short vowel; and it ends with ง (/**ng**/ as in *guarding)***:**

/**l**/ + /**a**/ + /**ng**/ = /**lang**/

/**gam**/-/**lang**/

Next, we calculate tone.

- **HDL**
- **HLR**
- **MDL**
- **MLM**
- **LDSH**
- **LDLF**
- **LLM**

Tone Rules

- Syllable 1: **M**iddle Class + **L**ive syllable = *mid tone* (**MLM**)
- Syllable 2: **L**ow Class + **L**ive syllable = *mid tone* (**LLM**)

กำลัง – gam-lang (it means *power, strength;* but is also used to indicate *continuous tense,* i.e. in the process of doing something).

Words in Context

Vowels and Tone Marks

are always written above the initial consonant (except in a cluster, when it's the second consonant).

ผมกำลังกินข้าว

You should be able to identify and read the first two words. See if you can work out the remainder (look for the vowels and tone marks to help you).

- The third word in this sentence is กิน

- The fourth word is ข้าว

These are very common words.

First, with กิน...

We can see the short vowel is written above the initial consonant and the final consonant is น. You should know these consonants, their sounds and classes:

$$/g/ + /i/ + /n/ = /gin/$$

(Remember the initial sound, this is <u>not</u> an alcoholic drink!)

Tone Rules

- HDL
- HLR
- MDL
- MLM
- LDSH
- LDLF
- LLM

Middle Class + Live syllable = *mid tone* (**MLM**)

กิน = gin (is a verb and means *to eat*)

Second, with ข้าว...

We haven't covered the vowel in the last word as yet, but you should recognise it: ข้าว.

We can work this word out from the initial consonant sound (/**k**/ as in **k**anga-roo); the long vowel (/**aa**/ as in p**a**lm); and, the final consonant, which makes the /**o**/ as in wave **o**ver sound when in the terminal position.

$$/k/ + /aa/ + /o/ = /kaao/$$

Tone Marks

The tone mark makes it easy for us:

High Class + Mái too (้) = *falling tone*

$$ข้าว = kâao (rice)$$

Though ข้าว means rice, in Thailand, as rice is eaten with most meals, ข้าว also has a general meaning of '*a meal*".

You may hear, กินข้าว which is, "gin kâao" meaning *"eat rice".* This basically means eat food.

Back to our example:

$$ผมกำลังกินข้าว$$

I + in the process of + eat + rice

It means:

"I am eating rice"

Example 3 - ประจำปี

Our last example in this section is ประจำปี

As always, we look for the vowels. You should be able to see three written here.

Now, this combination will either give us one 3-syllable word; two words with 2-syllables in one word and 1-syllable in the other; or three 1-syllable words – we just don't know at this stage. This is one of the difficulties of learning new vocabulary.

Let's break it down, what can we see?

Rule 5

สระ -ำ & สระ -ะ

always *mark the end of a syllable.*

Well, we can see สระ -ะ and สระ -ำ (which we know are both terminal vowels); and, the third vowel belongs to a syllable/word you encountered before (plus you should still be able to identify both the vowel and the word): the vowel is สระ -ี and the syllable/word is ปี.

It is quite possible that you may be trying to work out if there is an unwritten vowel between the ป and the ร at the front of the word (this is where you may think it could be a 4-syllable word) – and very commendable if you managed to see that – but, this is actually a **consonant cluster** (refer to Table 4 on page 17) and is actually quite common.

Consonant Clusters

always begin with

ก, ข, ค, ต, ป, ผ, or พ

*The second consonant is **always***

ร, ล, or ว

This particular cluster (ปร) is made up of /**bp**/ + /**r**/ and makes the diphthong /**bpr**/ sound. We encountered the initial consonant in the previous lesson and you will recall that the second consonant is **Low Class** and makes the /**r**/ sound when it is an initial consonant (/**r**/ as in *rabbit nibbling*).

Knowing this we can now work out the following:

ประ-จำ-ปี

At this point, it's dictionary time...

The first syllable is ประ, which has the short สระ -ะ vowel and is quite a common prefix. You will most likely encounter it (at first) in the word ประเทศ, which means *country*, *state* or *nation:*

- ประเทศไทย = Thailand (country Thai)
- ประเทศอังกฤษ = England (country England)

However, in this example it is a prefix for the second syllable จำ, which together form a 2-syllable word:

(/**bpra**/ + จำ) + ปี

The initial consonant of the second syllable is **Middle Class** จ, and it makes the /**j**/ as in *jabberwocky **t**ail* sound.

Again, we know this is an initial consonant as it has สระ -ะ before it and สระ -ำ after it, both of which always come after an initial consonant.

/**j**/ + /**am**/ = /**jam**/

This gives us:

(/**bpra**/ +/**jam**/) + ปี

As I said previously, this part comprises a 2-syllable word. The third 'part' (ปี)

has to be a single syllable/word and has the long vowel สิระ ◌ี (/ii/ as in

steeple) and a repeated **Middle Class** consonant (/**bp**/ as in *bottom **p**it*):

/**bp**/ + /**ii**/ = /**bpii**/

Together, they give us:

(/**bpra**/+/**jam**/) + /**bpii**/ = /**bpra**/-/**jam**/-/**bpii**/

Tone Rules

- HDL
- HLR
- MDL
- MLM
- LDSH
- LDLF
- LLM

We're never quite finished until we look at the syllable and word tone. There

aren't any tone marks in this word, so we have to calculate the tone of each

of the 3 syllables:

- Word 1, Syllable 1: **Middle Class** + **Dead syllable** = *low tone* (**MDL**)
- Word 1, Syllable 2: **Middle Class** + **Live syllable** = *mid tone* (**MLM**)
- Word 2: **Middle Class** + **Live syllable** = *mid tone* (**MLM**)

ประจำปี = bprà-jam bpi

As a 2-syllable word, ประจำ means *regularly,* or *frequently.* ปี means *year*

and is used as both a noun and as a classifier. When we combine them and

form a compound word, we get *regularly* + *year* = *annually*, or *yearly.*

Exercise 4

Exercise 4a

Answers start on page 343.

Match the words to their meaning:

1.	จะ	regularly	a.	
2.	ประเทศไทย	power, strength; in the process of doing something	b.	
3.	ข้าว	Male, personal pronoun, I	c.	
4.	ปี	year	d.	
5.	ทำ	England	e.	
6.	กำลัง	rice	f.	
7.	กิน	to eat rice	g.	
8.	ประจำ	annually	h.	
9.	ประเทศอังกฤษ	shall, will	i.	
10.	กินข้าว	shrimp paste	j.	
11.	ประจำปี	to eat	k.	
12.	กะปิ	to do, to make	l.	
13.	ผม	Thailand	m.	

Exercise 4b

Identify the syllables in these words (draw a vertical line, underline, or highlight the syllables):

1. กำจัด   4. นำเข้า

2. ทำงาน   5. ทำงานทำการ

3. สำหรับ   6. นำไปใช้

Practically all the Thai words used in this book come from the list of the 1176 most popular words used in the Thai language.

So, even though you may not know the vowels now, being able to recognise them and their syllables will benefit you later

Remember, we're trying to identify the syllable breaks in this exercise. If you remember the rules concerning where vowels are written, these shouldn't pose too many problems.

1. กำจัด – *to eradicate, to get rid of, to eliminate*

2. ทำงาน – *to work*

3. สำหรับ – *for, to*

4. นำเข้า – *to import, to introduce, to bring in*

5. ทำงานทำการ – *to do work*

6. นำไปใช้ – *to apply, to use, to utilise.*

Notes

สระ -า

We have already looked at the vowels that make the short /**a**/ sound (สระ -ะ and อ-). The vowel in this chapter, สระ -า, is the long vowel equivalent and makes the /**aa**/ as in *palm* sound.

As a final reminder about the Paiboon transliterated system, we 'double-up' on long vowels to clearly distinguish them from short vowels: /**aa**/ as opposed to /**a**/.

สระ -า is a long vowel for determining tone and, as we have already stated – and will state for the last time here – if no tone mark is present, we must determine whether a syllable is live or dead in order to calculate tone.

How is it used?

<u>All vowels must be associated with a consonant</u>; and, while English can have 'free-standing' vowels Thai cannot. As we've seen, this consonant can either be a single consonant or it can be a consonant cluster (a cluster is still classed as a single consonant even though both sounds are spoken).

สระ -า is always written **after** a consonant; but, what is important to note is there are no special rules surrounding this particular vowel: sometimes it will have a final consonant written after it, and sometimes it won't; as such, we must use other clues to help us.

We will now look at some word examples.

One Syllable Words

- ชาว

- ภาพ

- การ

- กา

- ขาย

- จาก

If you have a dictionary, you could of course look these words up; however, a good practice to get into is to always try and work out the pronunciation and tone first as the more you practice the better and faster at it you become.

Example 1 - ชาว

In this example, we see สระ -า is a medial vowel. It has a **Low Class** consonant either side of it: ช as an initial consonant, which makes the /ch/ as in **ch**ef *t*asting sound; and, ว in the final consonant position, which makes the /o/ as in w**a**ve **o**ver sound.

$$\text{/ch/ + /aa/ + /o/ = /chaao/}$$

- **HDL**
- **HLR**
- **MDL**
- **MLM**
- **LDSH**
- **LDLF**
- **LLM**

Tone Rule

There is no tone mark, so we must calculate tone:

Low Class + Live syllable = *mid tone* (**LLM**)

ชาว = **chaao** (it means *person)*

Example 2 - ภาพ

สระ -า is again a medial vowel with **Low Class** consonants ภ and พ either side of it. Both of these make the /**p**/ sound (/**p**/ as in **p**ainting and **p**raying, respectively).

$$/p/ + /aa/ + /p/ = /paap/$$

Tone Rules

Low Class + **D**ead syllable and **L**ong vowel = **f**alling tone (**LDLF**)

$$ภาพ = \textbf{pâap}\ (picture,\ photo)$$

Example 3 - การ

With **Middle Class** ก as an initial consonant we have the /**g**/ as in **g**alahad **k**night sound; and, with Low Class ร as the final consonant (/**n**/ as in rabbit **n**ibbling), this gives us:

$$/g/ + /aa/ + /n/ = /gaan/$$

Tone Rules

Middle Class + **L**ive syllable = **m**id tone (**MLM**)

การ = **gaan** (this word is used as a prefix before a verb to make it a noun –
a gerund)

Example 4 - กา

The long vowel is preceded by **Middle Class** ก as an initial consonant (again, this gives us the /**g**/ as in **g**alahad **k**night sound); this word is:

$$/g/ + /aa/ = /gaa/$$

- HDL
- HLR
- MDL
- MLM
- LDSH
- LDLF
- LLM

Tone Rules

Middle Class + **L**ive syllable = *mid tone* (**MLM**)

กา = **gaa** (when a noun, this means *kettle, crow, or teapot;* when used as a verb, it means *make a mark,* or *make a sign*).

Example 5 - ขาย

The long vowel สระ -า is preceded by **High Class** ข as the initial consonant (/**k**/ as in **k**angaroo); and, is followed by the **Low Class** final consonant ย, which makes the /**i**/ as in **y**eti **i**ce sound:

/**k**/ + /**aa**/ + /**i**/ = /**kaai**/

Tone Rules

High Class + **L**ive syllable = *rising tone* (**HLR**)

ขาย = **kǎai** (*to sell, to vend*)

Example 6 - จาก

Here we have two **Middle Class** consonants. As the initial consonant we have จ, which makes the /**j**/ as in **j**abberwocky **t**ail sound; and, as the final consonant, we have ก which makes the /**k**/ as in **g**alahad **k**night sound:

/**j**/ + /**aa**/ + /**k**/ = /**jaak**/

Tone Rules

Middle Class + **D**ead syllable = *low tone* (**MDL**)

จาก = **jàak** (it means *from, to depart, to leave, to go away from*).

Two Syllables/Words

- ขายของ

- จากไป

Again, you can look these up in a dictionary but try and work out the tone for each syllable/word before looking at the answers. The more you practice, the better you will get.

Example 7 - ขายของ

This is a *compound word* but we have already encountered and know the first word (page 94), it means *to sell*, *to vend*. The second part of this word-group is ของ.

We can see the initial consonant is **High Class** ข, which we know makes the /**k**/ as in *k*angaroo sound. The final consonant is **Low Class** ง which make the /**ng**/ as in guardi**ng** sound; however, what about อ, what is it doing here?

If you recall, this character can be a consonant or a vowel, and can perform a number of other functions (refer to "Silent Consonants" on page 33); but, in this instance, อ is acting as a vowel (สีระ -อ): if it was acting as a consonant (อ อ่าง) it would be the second of three consonants in this syllable; and, therefore would mean that ของ itself would be comprised of two syllables with no written vowels.

We already know that <u>every syllable must have a vowel</u> and this would necessitate two unwritten vowels – one either side of this consonant – and, therefore, อ has to be a vowel in this word, (สีระ -อ - /ɔɔ/ as in **aw**ful).

I hope you follow the logic here?

Including the first word ขาย, this compound word is comprised of:

/kǎai/ + /k/ + /ɔɔ/ + /ng/ = /kǎai/-/kɔɔng/

Tone Rules

- HDL
- HLR
- MDL
- MLM
- LDSH
- LDLF
- LLM

High Class + **L**ive syllable = *rising tone* (**HLR**)

ขายของ = **kǎai-kɔ̌ɔng** (*to sell goods*, to *make a sale*)

As I mentioned before, this is a compound word. ขาย on its own means *to sell*, and ของ on its own means *things*, or *possessions*: together, the word means *to sell things*, *sell goods*.

Example 8 - จากไป

We haven't covered สระ ไ- yet, but you should know that this vowel makes the /ai/ as in *fly* sound. We looked at the first word on page 94, so the second syllable/word has to be ไป.

Rule 4

Sà-rà ไ-, ใ-, -ะ
and -̊า *are **never** followed by a final consonant.*

สระ ไ- is always written in front of an initial consonant (rule 4, page 44); and once again, this clue helps us break sentences and words down into their component parts.

Rule 1

The consonant is always pronounced first.

For the consonant sound, ป is a **Middle Class** consonant which makes the /**bp**/ diphthong sound when it is in the initial consonant position (you should recall a man in the *bottom pit)*. We now have

/jàak/ + /ai/ + /bp/

The consonant is always pronounced first (rule 1), so we rearrange the vowel and the consonant to give us:

$$/jàak/ + /bp/ + /ai/ = /jàak/-/bpai/$$

Tone Rules

- HDL
- HLR
- MDL
- MLM
- LDSH
- LDLF
- LLM

Middle Class + **L**ive syllable = *mid tone* (**MLM**)

 จากไป = **jàak-bpai** (*to depart*, *to go away from*)

จาก on it's own means *from*, *depart*, etc. The second part, ไป, on its own has one common meaning as a verb: *to go*, *to leave*, and *to depart*.

Three syllables/words

- สถานี

- การศึกษา

Example 9 – สถานี

For the first example in this section, we can identify three consonants and two written vowels.

As this word has 3-syllables (it is in the 3-syllable section after all), we know there has to be an unwritten vowel somewhere; but, if this word wasn't in this particular section, how would we know this and how could we break-down this word? The answer is simple. As always, we look for the vowels.

First, at the very end of the word we see the long vowel สระ ◌ี (/**ii**/ as in *steeple*) written above **Low Class** น (/**n**/ as in *navigating*). We know vowels written above a consonant are always written above the initial consonant. This identifies the end syllable:

สถา-นี

$$สถา - /n/ + /ii/ = สถา-/nii/$$

Moving left, towards the beginning of the word, we next see the long vowel สระ -า written after the initial **High Class** consonant ถ (/t/ as in *tai*ls); this is either the middle syllable, or ส and ถ would have to form a consonant cluster at the start of the syllable/word.

Well, the only way to know the consonant clusters is to learn them (refer to Table 4 on page 17 if you haven't got them off to a tee yet). After we have done that, we know that ส never forms consonant clusters and must, therefore, be an initial consonant; and, as we can't see a vowel - and every syllable has to have one - the vowel for this syllable has to be unwritten.

Consonant Clusters

always begin with

ก, ข, ค, ต, ป, ผ, or พ

*The second consonant is **always***

ร, ล, or ว

$$ส-ถา-นี$$

Taking this one step further, if this first syllable did have a final, or terminal consonant, then the unwritten vowel would naturally be between two consonants in the **same syllable** (/o/); but, as there is no terminal consonant in this syllable, the unwritten vowel must be between two consonants in **different syllables** (/a/). This gives us:

$$/s/ + /a/ + /t/ + /aa/ - /nii/$$

Or, more specifically by syllable (which is what we need):

$$/sa/-/taa/-/nii/$$

Tone Rules

- HDL
- HLR
- MDL
- MLM
- LDSH
- LDLF
- LLM

- Syllable 1: **H**igh Class + **D**ead syllable = *low tone* (**HDL**)
- Syllable 2: **H**igh Class + **L**ive syllable = *rising tone* (**HLR**)
- Syllable 3: **L**ow Class + **L**ive syllable = *mid tone* (**LLM**)

สถานี = **sà-tăa-nii** (*station*)

The Thai word for railway is รถไฟ and you have encountered all but the last consonant here; however, you should know this consonant, the sounds it makes, and the consonant class. I hope you can work it out.

Putting these together we get:

สถานีรถไฟ (*railway station*)

Example 10 – การศึกษา

As always, look for the written vowels. Here we can see three of them: สระ -า, สระ -ึ, and สระ -า.

We can start at the front as we know the word /**gaan**/:

/**gaan**/ + ศึกษา

Vowels and Tone Marks
are always written above the initial consonant (except in a cluster, when it's the second consonant).

The next consonant is High Class consonant ศ, (/**s**/ as in **s**ign **t**op); and. it has a vowel written above it. The vowel sound is /**ʉ**/ as in p**u**sh-up and we know it's a short vowel. The terminal consonant in this syllable is ก, which makes the /**k**/ as in galahad **k**night sound:

/**gaan**/ + /**sʉk**/ + ษา

Our third syllable begins with another High Class consonant ษ (/s/ as in *sea trip*) and is followed by long vowel สีระ -า. We now have:

/gaan/ + /sʉk/ + /saa/

Tone Rules

- HDL
- HLR
- MDL
- MLM
- LDSH
- LDLF
- LLM

- Syllable 1: **M**iddle Class + **L**ive syllable = *mid tone* (**MLM**)
- Syllable 2: **H**igh Class + **D**ead syllable = *low tone* (**HDL**)
- Syllable 3: **H**igh Class + **L**ive syllable = *rising tone* (**HLR**)

การศึกษา = gaan-sʉk-sǎa *(education, study or learning)*

As we discussed earlier, การ is used as a prefix before a verb to make it a noun (a gerund). The word ศึกษา (sʉk-sǎa) is a verb meaning *to study*, or *to learn*.

การ is used as a prefix before a verb to make it a noun (a gerund)

On occasion, you will also encounter the prefix นัก (nák); this is sometimes used before verbs to describe that noun as a profession. For example, if you saw นักศึกษา (nák-sʉk-sǎa), this means *the profession of learning* or *studying = student*.

Therefore, from the one core word ศึกษา, we have:

- ศึกษา = *to study, to learn*
- นักศึกษา = *student* or *learner*
- การศึกษา = *education, study, learning*.

Exercise 5

Exercise 5a

Answers start on page 344.

Match the words to their meaning:

1.	กา (n)	to sell, to vend	a.
2.	สถานี	to depart, to go away from	b.
3.	การศึกษา	teapot, kettle, crow	c.
4.	นักศึกษา	person	d.
5.	สถานีรถไฟ	turns a verb into a gerund	e.
6.	ภาพ	station	f.
7.	กา (v)	student, learner	g.
8.	ชาว	railway station	h.
9.	รถไฟ	from, to depart, to leave, to go away from	i.
10.	จากไป	to make a mark, to make a sign	j.
11.	การ	please	k.
12.	ขาย	education, study, learning	l.
13.	กรุณา	railway	m.
14.	จาก	photo, picture	n

Exercise 5b

Identify the syllables in these words (draw a vertical line, underline, or high-light the syllables):

1. ชำนาญ   4. รักษา

2. ทำลาย   5. น้ำมัน

3. น้ำแข็ง   6. สะพาน

Their meaning:

1. ชำนาญ – *[is] experienced, skilled, expert, adroit*

2. ทำลาย – *to damage, to do harm, to destroy*

3. น้ำแข็ง – *ice*

4. รักษา – *to take care of, to save, to maintain, to treat, to cure*

5. น้ำมัน – *oil, fuel, gasoline*

6. สะพาน – *bridge, pier.*

Applying the rules for reading Thai will help you identify the individual sylla-bles of these compound words and these extra words, though not in any context, will also help expand your vocabulary.

Notes

สระ เ-

สระ เ- makes the /**ee**/ as in *bed* sound. It is a long vowel for pronunciation and tone rule purposes.

How is it used?

สระ เ- is **always** written before an initial consonant and **always** identifies the start of a syllable or word. This is another simple rule to help us *immediately* and quickly identify where a syllable or word begins.

One Syllable Words

- เลข
- เล่น
- เก่ง
- เต้น
- เป็น

Example 1 - เลข

We know this vowel is always written before a consonant and we know the initial consonant for this word is ล, a **Low Class** consonant, which makes the /l/ as in *l*arge *n*ugget sound. The final consonant is **High Class** ข, which makes the /k/ as in *k*angaroo sound irrespective of whether it is an initial or a final consonant. This gives us:

/ee/ + /l/ + /k/

Rule 1

The consonant is always pronounced first.

Regardless of where the consonant is written it is always pronounced first; this becomes:

/l/ + /ee/ + /k/ = /leek/

Tone Rules

- HDL
- HLR
- MDL
- MLM
- LDSH
- LDLF
- LLM

Low Class + **D**ead syllable and **L**ong vowel = *falling tone* (**LDLF**)

เลข = lêek *(numeral, number, digit)*

Remember the pronunciation, don't pronounce this word like a Welsh vegetable!

Example 2 - เล่น

There are two differences between เล่น and the previous word: the final consonant (/n/ as in *n*avigating) and the tone mark Mái èek:

/l/ + /ee/ + /n/ = /leen/

Tone Mark

When there's a tone mark it overrides all other rules:

Low Class + Mái èek (˘-) = *falling tone*

เล่น = lêen (*to play*)

Example 3 - เก่ง

With เก่ง, the initial consonant is **Middle Class** (ก) (/**g**/ as in *galahad knight*), and the final consonant is **Low Class** ง (/**ng**/ as in *guardi**ng***).

/**g**/ + /**ee**/ + /**ng**/ = /**geeng**/

Tone Mark

Middle Class consonant + Mái èek = *low tone*.

เก่ง = gèeng (*to be good at something*)

Example 4 - เต้น

In the next example, เต้น, there are three changes: 1) **Middle Class** ต, which as an initial consonant makes the /**dt**/ as in *damsel tower* sound (remember, this is different from the /**d**/ sound that ด makes); 2) **Low Class** น is the final consonant, making the /**n**/ as in ***n**avigating* sound; and, 3) we have Mái too as the tone mark:

/**dt**/ + /**ee**/ + /**n**/ = /**dteen**/

Tone Marks

Middle Class + Mái too (˝-) = *falling tone*

เต้น = dtêen (*to dance*)

Example 5 - เป็น

ไม้ไต่คู้

Mái-dtài-kúu (◌็) is used to shorten certain vowels, such as:

สระ เ-

and

สระ แ-.

This example differs slightly as เป็น has a symbol above the initial consonant. This symbol ◌็, is called Mái-dtài-kúu (ไม้ไต่คู้) and it is used to shorten certain vowels. One such vowel is สระ เ- which, though it is usually written as /**ee**/, is shortened to /**e**/ when Mái-dtài-kúu is above it.

We have **Middle Class** ป as the initial consonant (making the /**bp**/ as in **b**ottom **p**it sound); and, **Low Class** น as the terminal/final consonant (/**n**/ as in **n**avigating).

Without Mái-dtài-kúu the word would be:

/**bp**/ + /**ee**/ + /**n**/

But with it, the vowel is:

/**bp**/ + /**e**/ + /**n**/

- HDL
- HLR
- MDL
- MLM
- LDSH
- LDLF
- LLM

Tone Rules

Mái-dtài-kúu has a strict function, it is **not** a tone mark and normal tone rules apply:

Middle Class + **L**ive syllable = *mid tone* (**MLM**)

เป็น = bpen (*to be*)

What is the Purpose of Mái-dtài-kúu?

You may be thinking why don't we just write สระ เ-ะ as it will produce exactly the same vowel sound?

Yes, it will produce the same sound; but, there are 2 main things happenig here: 1) it's all about the tone. If we used the short vowel สระ เ-ะ, then this would create a dead syllable and we would have to apply **MDL** instead of **MLM**. As we know, with a tonal language, if you change the tone you also change the word and its meaning. 2) There cannot be a final consonant after any vowel containing สระ -ะ; it is a terminal vowel.

Let's look at how we use the word เป็น:

ผมเป็นคนไทย

You have encountered three of these words already and the fourth means *person*.

Pŏm bpen kon tai

I am person Thai

(or, *I am Thai*).

If you replace ไทย with the country you are from, this is how you tell some-one your nationality:

- For an English man... ผมเป็นคนอังกฤษ (*I am English*)

- A Canadian man would say: ผมเป็นคนแคนาดา (*I am Canadian*)

- Whereas a Canadian woman would say: ดิฉันเป็นคนแคนาดา (*I am Canadian*)

Two Syllables/words:

- เช่นกัน

- ประเทศ

- เวลา

Example 6 - เช่นกัน

In เช่นกัน, a 2-syllable word, we're not seeing anything new. You can see two vowels, one in each syllable/word: the long vowel in the first, and Mái Hăn-aa-gàat (อั-) in the second.

The first syllable/word is made up of **Low Class** ช as an initial consonant (/**ch**/ as in **ch**ef *tasting*), and น as the terminal consonant (/**n**/ as in **n**avigating):

/**ch**/ + /**ee**/ + /**n**/ = /**cheen**/

The second syllable/word has **Middle Class** ก as an initial consonant (/**g**/ as in **g**alahad *knight*), Mái Hăn-aa-gàat as the medial vowel (/**a**/), and *navigating* as the final consonant:

/**cheen**/ + /**g**/ + /**a**/ + /**n**/ = /**cheen**/-/**gan**/

- HDL
- HLR
- MDL
- MLM
- LDSH
- LDLF
- LLM

Tone

- Syllable 1: Low Class + Mái èek (-่) = *falling tone*
- Syllable 2: **M**iddle Class + **L**ive syllable = *mid tone* (**MLM**)

เช่นกัน = chêen-gan (it means *same*)

Example 7 - ประเทศ

We did talk about ประเทศ briefly before, but having worked this far, I hope it is clear that by locating the vowels already discussed, we can see two syllables in this word.

We see สระ -ะ, which is a terminal vowel and <u>always</u> marks the end of a syllable or word; and, we can see สระ เ- which, as we know, is always written before an initial consonant.

We encountered this first syllable/word before, it is a common prefix and is comprised of a consonant cluster, made up of **Middle Class** ป (*/bp/* as in *bottom pit*) and **Low Class** ร (*/r/* as in *rabbit nibbling*), and สระ -ะ:

$$/bpr/ + /a/ = /bpra/$$

The second syllable/word is comprised of Low Class ท (*/t/* as in *typist*) and High Class ศ (*/t/* as in *sign top* as a terminal consonant):

$$/t/ + /ee/ + /t/ = /teet/$$

Tone Rules

- Syllable 1: **M**iddle Class + **D**ead syllable = *low tone* (**MDL**)
- Syllable 2: **L**ow Class + **D**ead syllable and **L**ong vowel = *falling tone* (**LDLF**)

$$ประเทศ = bpra-têet \ (country)$$

Referring back to our earlier example of using language, when we said "*I am Thai*" (or English, or Canadian); we would use ประเทศ to say, "*I come from...*" For example:

ผมมาจากประเทศไทย

There is one word here that you haven't encountered: มา (it is a verb and means *to come*).

มา is comprised of **Low Class** ม (/**m**/ as in *map*) and long vowel สระ -า.

When มา is used with จาก, which we know means *from*, they join to mean *come from* (มาจาก)

ผมมาจากประเทศไทย

Pǒm maa-jàak bprà-têet tai

I come from Thailand

Example 8 - เวลา

In example 8, you can quite clearly see two long vowels and the two syllables to which they 'belong'.

The first syllable has สระ เ- (/**ee**/) and **Low Class** consonant ว as an initial consonant (/**w**/ as in *wave over*); and, the second syllable has **Low Class** ล as an initial consonant (/**l**/ as in *large nugget*), and the written long vowel สระ-า (/**aa**/ as in *palm*). This gives us:

/**w**/ + /**ee**/ + /**l**/ + /**aa**/ = /**wee**/-/**laa**/

- HDL
- HLR
- MDL
- MLM
- LDSH
- LDLF
- LLM

Tone Rules

- Syllable 1: Low Class + Live syllable = *mid tone* (**LLM**)
- Syllable 2: Low Class + Live syllable = *mid tone* (**LLM**)

เวลา = wee-laa (*time*)

Exercise 6

Exercise 6a

Answers begin on page 344

Match the words to their meaning:

1.	ศึกษา	Canada	a.
2.	จาก	numeral, number, digit	b.
3.	เต้น	turns a verb into a noun (a gerund)	c.
4.	คน	education	d.
5.	เวลา	to be	e.
6.	ประเทศ	to come	f.
7.	เล่น	to study, to learn	g.
8.	มา	same	h.
9.	แคนาดา	time	i.
10.	เป็น	to dance	j.
11.	มาจาก	from	k.
12.	การศึกษา	country	l.
13.	การ	classifier for person	m.
14.	เช่นกัน	to play	n
15.	เลข	to come from	o

Exercise 6b

Identify the syllables in these words (draw a vertical line, underline, or highlight the syllables):

1. จำเป็น   4. เมล็ด   7. รางวัล

2. ประมาณ   5. ระหว่าง   8. รู้จัก

3. เมตตา   6. รับประทาน   9. สำนัก

Their meaning:

1. จำเป็น – *necessary, essential, required*

2. ประมาณ – *approximately, about, roughly*

3. เมตตา – *goodwill, kindness, mercy, compassion*

4. เมล็ด – *seed, grain, tiny piece*

5. ระหว่าง – *between, in the middle of, among*

6. รับประทาน – *to dine, to eat, to have a meal, to sup*

7. รางวัล – *award, prize, reward*

8. รู้จัก – *to know (a person, or place)*

9. สำนัก – *office, institute, bureau.*

Notes

สระ แ- makes the /ɛɛ/ as in *mare* sound and is a long vowel for pronunciation and tone rule purposes.

How is it used?

สระ แ- is always written before an initial consonant and, as in the previous chapter (สระ เ-), provides us with a clear and simple way of identifying where a syllable or word starts and ends.

One Syllable Words

- แม่
- แก่
- แก้
- แฟน
- แยก

Example 1 - แม่

In this first example, we see long vowel สระ แ- written at the start of the word, directly in front of the only consonant, **Low Class** ม (/m/ as in *map*):

$$/m/ + /ɛɛ/ = /mɛɛ/$$

Tone Mark

Low Class + Mái èek = *falling tone*

$$แม่ = mêε \text{ (mother)}$$

Example 2 - แก่

In example 2, we have a change of consonant to Middle Class ก (/**g**/ as in **g**alahad **k**night):

$$/g/ + /εε/ = /gεε/$$

Tone Mark

Middle Class + Mái èek = *low tone*

$$แก่ = gèε \text{ (to be old, or elderly)}$$

Example 3 - แก้

The only change here is the tone mark.

Tone Mark

Middle Class + Mái too = *falling tone*

$$แก้ = gêε \text{ (to fix, to solve, to rectify)}$$

Example 4 - แฟน

Now we see two Low Class consonants: ฟ as an initial consonant (/**f**/ as in **f**inished **p**icking); and, น as the final consonant (/**n**/ as in **n**avigating):

$$/f/ + /εε/ + /n/ = /fεεn/$$

- HDL
- HLR
- MDL
- MLM
- LDSH
- LDLF
- LLM

Tone Rules

Low Class + Live syllable = *mid tone* (**LLM**)

แฟน = fɛɛn *(girlfriend/boyfriend, or partner)*

Example 5 - แยก

Now we have **Low Class** ย in the initial consonant position (/**y**/ as in **y**eti **i**ce); and, we have Middle Class ก in the final/terminal consonant position (/**k**/ as in **g**alahad **k**night).

$$/y/ + /\varepsilon\varepsilon/ + /k/ = /y\varepsilon\varepsilon k/$$

Tone Rules

Low Class + Dead syllable and Long vowel = *falling tone* (**LDLF**)

แยก = yɛ̂ɛk *(to divide, to separate, to part)*

Two or More Syllables/Words

- แล้ว

- แล้วก็

- แม่น้ำ

- แม่น้ำแม่กลอง

- แบบนี้

Example 6 - แล้ว

In the word แล้ว, we have long vowel สระ แ-, tone mark Mái too, and Low

Class ล in the initial consonant position (/l/ as in *large nugget*); and, ว in the

final position (/o/ as in *wave over*):

/l/ + /ɛɛ/ + /o/ = /lɛɛo/

Tone Mark

Low Class + Mái too = *high tone*

แล้ว= lέεo (it is used as a marker to

indicate that the action has already occurred)

For example, กินแล้ว, *[I've] eaten already*

Example 7 - แล้วก็

In our second two syllable/word example, the first part is the same as that

just covered; and, the second part/syllable is the addition of Middle Class ก.

Is ก an initial or a final consonant here?

ไม้ไต่คู้

Mái-dtài-kúu (ั) is used to shorten certain vowels.

I hope you remember the symbol above the Middle Class consonant; we

looked at it before, it's called Mái-dtài-kúu (ไม้ไต่คู้) and it is used to shorten

certain vowels.

With just one exception, Mái-dtài-kúu must have a written vowel after it, the

syllable cannot just end with (็ -); this one exception is ก็.

The Inherent Vowel
*The inherent vowel makes the /ɔɔ/ as in **aw**ful sound. Every consonant has this.*

ก็ is pronounced with the inherent (อ) vowel sound (page 20); but, in the

same way as /ee/ was shortened to /e/ in the earlier example, Mái-dtài-kúu

shortens สระ -อ (/ɔɔ/) to สระ เ-าะ (/ɔ/). This syllable/word makes the following sound:

$$\textbf{/g/} + \textbf{/ɔ/} = \textbf{/gɔ/}.$$

With the first syllable/word, we now have:

แล้ว - **/gɔ/**

Tone

We have already calculated the first part in the previous example. The second part, ก็, is actually a *reduced form* of the vowel เ-าะ plus Mai too (-ฺ);
and, as such:

Middle Class + Mái too = *falling tone*

Refer to Appendix G - Modifying Vowels on page 338 for more detail on different forms and modifying vowels.

แล้วก็ = lɛ́ɛo-gɔ̂ (*and then, and after that*)

ผมต้องการอันนี้แล้วก็อันนั้น

- ต้องการ – *to want, to need, to require*
- อันนี้ – *this one*
- อันนั้น – *that one*

   I would like this one and also that one.

Example 8 - แม่น้ำ

Example 8 is slightly easier and here we see the first syllable/word as being the same word for 'mother' (example 1 in this section); the second word is the Thai word for water with Low Class น in the initial consonant position (/**n**/ as in **n**avigating), followed by สระ -ำ, which makes the /**am**/ as in **um**brella sound:

แม่ + /**n**/ + /**am**/ = แม่ - /**nam**/

Tone Mark

Low Class + Mái too = *high tone*

แม่น้ำ = mɛ̂ɛ-nám (separately, the words mean
mother-water, together they mean *river*).

Example 9 - แม่น้ำแม่กลอง

Example 9 builds on the previous แม่น้ำ example, and is the name of a river. It is where the authors went on a short trip outside of Bangkok just before Songkran 2013. Let's look at the name แม่กลอง.

Consonant Clusters

always begin with
ก, ข, ค, ต, ป, ผ, or พ

*The second consonant is **always***
ร, ล, or ว

We know the first syllable (after แม่น้ำ), as we've already encountered it twice in this section (แม่); and, at first glance, this leaves us 4 consonants in the second syllable/word.

First thoughts are that there could be a number of unwritten vowels here and you may either have to ask someone or, at the very least reach, for your trusty dictionary. However, when you remember that ก (/**g**/ as in **g**alahad knight) is a Middle Class consonant that can form consonant clusters, and the second consonant ล is a **Low Class** consonant with which it can form clusters (/l/ as in *large* **n***ugget)*, it may make it easier.

Also, when you remember that อ can be a consonant and a vowel (obviously not at the same time) you can see that this syllable does actually have a written vowel and all the parts of this particular puzzle start to fall neatly into place.

สระ -อ

Often when you encounter อ in the middle of 2 other consonants, it will be acting as a vowel.

Now, you can clearly see that Low Class ง is the final consonant in a syllable comprised of a consonant cluster, a written vowel, and a final consonant:

$$(/g/ + /l/) + /ɔɔ/ + /ng/ = /glɔɔng/$$

Putting it all together, the whole word makes /mɛ̂ɛ-nám/ + /mɛ̂ɛ/-/**glɔɔng**/

Tone Rules

- HDL
- HLR
- MDL
- MLM
- LDSH
- LDLF
- LLM

- Word 1, syllable 1: Low Class + Mái èek = *falling tone*
- Word 1, syllable 2: Low Class + Mái too = *high tone*
- Word 2, syllable 1: Low Class + Mái èek = *falling tone*
- Word 2, syllable 2: **M**iddle Class + **L**ive syllable = *mid tone* (**MLM**)

แม่น้ำแม่กลอง = mɛ̂ɛ-nám mɛ̂ɛ-glɔɔng
(river *Mɛ̂ɛ-glɔɔng*, or *Mɛ̂ɛ-glɔɔng river*).

Example 10 - แบบนี้

Vowels and Tone Marks
are always written above the initial consonant (except in a cluster, when it's the second consonant).

We can see two written vowels in this example and though we haven't covered the second vowel as yet, we have encountered it before; and, we also know that with the exception of consonant clusters, vowels written above a consonant are always written above the first consonant in a syllable (as a further clue, น never forms consonants clusters).

Simple Vowels   123

For our first syllable we have สระ แ- followed by Middle Class บ as an initial consonant (/**b**/ as in **b**ald **p**atch); and, then we have the same consonant in the final consonant position, where it makes the /**p**/ sound:

$$/b/ + /\varepsilon\varepsilon/ + /p/ = /b\varepsilon\varepsilon p/$$

In our second syllable, we have Low Class น, long vowel สระ ◌ี (/**ii**/ as in st**ee**ple), and Mái too:

$$/n/ + /ii/ = / nii/$$

Together, these make:

$$/b\varepsilon\varepsilon p/ + /nii/ = /b\varepsilon\varepsilon p\text{-}nii/$$

- HDL
- HLR
- MDL
- MLM
- LDSH
- LDLF
- LLM

Tone Rules

- Syllable 1: **M**iddle Class + **L**ive syllable = *mid tone* (**MLM**)

- Syllable 2: Low Class + Mái too = *high tone*

    แบบนี้ = bɛɛp-níi *(like this, this way)*

Exercise 7

Exercise 7a

Answers begin on page 344

Match the words to their meaning:

1.	แฟน	old, elderly	a.
2.	แล้ว	and after that, and then	b.
3.	แก้	to work	c.
4.	กรุณา	river	d.
5.	แยก	good at something	e.
6.	คนไทย	girlfriend/boyfriend, or partner	f.
7.	แบบนี้	annually	g.
8.	แม่	to divide, to separate, to part	h.
9.	แล้วก็	indicates action has already occurred	i.
10.	แม่น้ำ	a Thai person	j.
11.	แก่	ice	k.
12.	ทำงาน	to fix, to solve, to rectify	l.
13.	เก่ง	mother	m.
14.	น้ำแข็ง	like this, this way	n
15.	ประจำปี	please	o

Exercise 7b

Identify the syllables in these words (draw a vertical line, underline, or highlight the syllables):

1. แข็งแรง   4. แม้แต่   7. แนะนำ

2. แล้วแต่   5. แทบจะ   8. แผ่นดิน

3. แทนที่   6. แทนที่จะ   9. แพงมาก

Their meaning:

1. แข็งแรง – *strong, solid, firm-like*

2. แล้วแต่ – *to depend on*

3. แทนที่ – *to replace, to substitute, to take place of*

4. แม้แต่ – *even* (conjunction)

5. แทบจะ – *almost, nearly, just about*

6. แทนที่จะ – *instead of*

7. แนะนำ – *to introduce, to suggest, to advise, to direct*

8. แผ่นดิน – *land, country, kingdom, ground, earth, plot of land*

9. แพงมาก – *very expensive.*

Notes

Shortening Vowels

In สระ -ะ & อ้-, beginning on page 67, we mentioned that one of the purposes of สระ -ะ is to shorten certain vowels; and, whenever you see สระ -ะ at the end of a syllable or word which also contains a long vowel, then สระ -ะ will shorten that long vowel.

สระ แ- (/εε/) is one of these vowels. The shortened version of สระ แ- is สระ แ-ะ, and the sound it makes is /ε/ as in *trap*. สระ เ- is another and adding สระ -ะ creates short vowel สระ เ-ะ, which makes the /e/ as in *net* sound.

Example 1 - เตะ

Here we see สระ เ-ะ and the Middle Class consonant ต (/**dt**/ as in *d*amsel *t*ower):

- HDL
- HLR
- MDL
- MLM
- LDSH
- LDLF
- LLM

$$/\text{dt}/ + /\text{e}/ = /\text{dte}/$$

Tone Rules

Middle Class + **D**ead syllable = *low tone* (**MDL**)

เตะ = dtè *(to kick)*

Example 2 - และ

Now we have Low Class consonant ล, (/l/ as in *large nugget)*, with สระ

แ-ะ:

$$/l/ + /ɛ/ = /lɛ/$$

Tone Rules

- HDL
- HLR
- MDL
- MLM
- LDSH
- LDLF
- LLM

Low Class + **D**ead syllable and **S**hort vowel = *high tone* (**LDSH**)

แล:ะ = lɛ́ *(and)*

สระ เ- and สระ แ- are the most common vowels that are shortened by

สระ -ะ. Other vowels shortened are:

- Simple vowels:

  — สระ โ-ะ (/o/ as in *cot*) - this is the unwritten /o/ we use.

  — สระ เ-าะ (/ɔ/ as in *slot*) [6]

- Complex vowels:

  — สระ เ-อะ (/ə/ as in *above*)

  — สระ เ-ียะ (/ia/ as in *ria*)

  — สระ เ-ือะ (/ʉa/ as in *newer*)

  — สระ -ัวะ (/ua/ as in *buat*).

These four complex vowels are extremely rare.

---

6. สระ โ-ะ and สระ เ-าะ sound very similar and are almost indistinguishable in English
   pronunciation.

Example 3 – เกาะ

This word is commonly seen in your trips to the islands of Thailand. We have Middle Class ก and สระ เ-าะ ($/ɔ/$ as in *slot*):

$$/g/ + /ɔ/ = /gɔ/$$

Tone Rules

Middle Class + **D**ead syllable = *low tone* (**MDL**)

เกาะ = gɔ̀ (it can be a noun meaning *island;*

and, it can be a verb meaning *to hold*).

สระ ไ- & ใ-

In this chapter we will look at the two vowels that make the /ai/ sound: สระ ไ- (sà-rà ai mái-má-lai, **ai** as in *fly*) and สระ ใ- (sà-rà ai mái-múuan, **ai** as in *knight*). They both make exactly the same sound but we need to use 2 different pictures and names to aid memory.

How are they used?

These two vowels are always written before an initial consonant (and never followed by a final consonant – rule 4) and this is another instant way of identifying where a syllable or word begins.

The difference between these two vowels is that สระ ใ- is only used by 20 words in the Thai language:

- ใช่ (châi - *yes*)
- ใช้ (chái - *to use*)
- ใคร (krai - *who*)
- ใคร่ (krâi - *to desire*)
- ใส (săi - *clear*)
- ใส่ (sài - *to put in*)
- ใบ (bai - *leaf*)

- ใบ้ (bâi - *mute, dumb*)
- ได (dai - *any*)
- ใต้ (dtâi - *south, underneath*)
- ใน (nai - *in*)
- ใฝ่ (fài - *aim*)
- ใกล้ (glâi - *near, close*)

- ใย (yai - *web, fibre*)
- ให้ (hâi - *to give, to let, to permit*)
- ใหญ่ (yài - *big, large*)
- สะใภ้ (sà-pái - *daughter in law*)
- ใหม่ (mài - *new, again*)
- หลง-ใหล (lŏng-lăi - *fascinating*)

Of course, reading these is easy, but when it comes to writing them, you just have to remember all 20; naturally, สระ ใ- is more common.

One Syllable Words

- ไก่
- ไข่
- ได้
- ไต่

- ไม่
- ไป
- ไหม

Example 1 – ไก่

The first example should be quite familiar to you now. It consists of sà-rà ai mái-má-lai (สระ ไ-), and **Middle Class** ก (/**g**/ as in **g**alahad **k**night):

$$/g/ + /ai/ = \textbf{gai}$$

Tone Mark

Middle Class + Mái èek = *low tone*

$$ไก่ = gài \text{ (it means \textit{chicken})}$$

Example 2 - ไข่

Next, we see the consonant has changed to High Class ข (/**k**/ as in **k**anga-roo). This combination gives us:

$$/k/ + /ai/ = \textbf{kai}$$

Tone Mark

High Class + Mái èek = *low tone*

ไข่ = kài (*egg*)

Example 3 - ได้

Here we have **Middle Class** ด (/**d**/ as in **d**amsel **t**ower), Mái too, and sà-rà ai mái-má-lai:

/**d**/ + /**ai**/ = **dai**

Tone Mark

Middle Class + Mái too = *falling tone*

ได้ = dâi (it has two meanings:
1) as an auxiliary verb meaning *can*, or *be able to;* and,
2) as a verb meaning *to get, to receive*).

Example 4 - ไต่

dt versus d
Don't mistake the
/**dt**/ *sound with the*
/**d**/ *sound, they are*
quite different.

Don't forget, this consonant makes the diphthong /**dt**/ as in **d**amsel **t**ower sound, which together with Mái èek and sà-rà ai mái-má-lai gives us:

/**dt**/ + /**ai**/ = **dtai**

Tone Mark

Middle Class + Mái èek = *low tone*

ไต่ = dtài *(to climb)*

Example 5 - ไม่

Here we have **Low Class** ม which makes the /**m**/ as in *map* sound, plus our tone mark Mái èek and sà-rà ai mái-má-lai:

/**m**/ + /**ai**/ = **mai**

Tone Mark

Low Class + Mái èek = *falling tone*

ไม่ = mâi *(no, not)*

Example 6 – ไป

- HDL
- HLR
- MDL
- MLM
- LDSH
- LDLF
- LLM

In this example, we see **Middle Class** ป (/**bp**/ as in *bottom pit*) with สระ ไ-:

/**bp**/ + /**ai**/ = **bpai**

Tone Rules

Middle Class + Live syllable = *mid tone* (**MLM**)

ไป = bpai *(to go)*

Example 7 – ไหม

Example 7 is slightly different as we have two consonants written immediately after the vowel. At this stage I hope you're either trying to see if there is either an unwritten vowel here, whether there is a consonant cluster, or maybe you remember that ห can be a preceding consonant?

As it turns out, it's the latter role. Immediately after silent ห we see **Low**

Class ม, (/**m**/ as in *map*) and know that ห is performing its silent role to

change the tone of this word:

/**silent**/ + /**m**/ + /**ai**/ = /<u>**mai**</u>/

Are ห or อ acting as a Preceding Consonant?

Another clue to seeing the role of ห or อ is whether the next consonant is

Low Class. If it isn't, then neither ห nor อ will be acting as a preceding con-

sonant: the function of silent consonants is to enable *low* or *rising tone* with

Low Class consonants (refer to Appendix E - Preceding Consonants).

Tone Rules

High Class + Live syllable = *rising tone* (**HLR**)

ไหม = mǎi (this word is a 'question word' and is used

to turn a statement into a question)

Real-life Example

A common greeting after you've said สวัสดี is to ask the person how they

are. You would ask:

สบายดีไหม

สบายดี = sà-baai-dii on its own is a compound word which

means *fine*.

As we said, the use of ไหม at the end of a sentence turns the statement into

a question; in English, we'd replace ไหม with a question mark:

สบายดีไหม = สบายดี**?**

We now have:

"*You are well?*"

The answer to this is usually either สบายดี (which is a statement that *I am fine/well);* or, we prefix the answer with ไม่ (mâi, which means *no,* to negate it:

ไม่สบาย = mâi sà-baai.

ไม่สบาย is a verb and means *to be unwell,* or *to be ill.*

We now have 2 words, which though they may sound similar to a non-Thai are quite different words to those with an attuned ear: ไม่ *(falling tone)* and ไหม *(rising tone).*

Two Syllables/Words (or more)

- ทำไม

- เท่าไร

- เมื่อไร

- ไปรษณีย์

Example 8 - ทำไม

This example contains two **Low Class** consonants, *(/*t*/ as in *typist* and /m/ as in *map),* plus two written vowels, both of which are known to you. This example is:

/t/ + /am/ + /m/ + /ai/ = /tam-mai/

Tone Rules

- Low Class + Live syllable = *mid tone* (**LLM**)
- Low Class + Live syllable = *mid tone* (**LLM**)

ทำไม = tam-mai (this is another question word which means *why?*)

Example 9 - เท่าไร

We haven't covered the first vowel yet; but, hopefully you can remember that it makes the **/ao/** as in *mouse* sound.

The composition of this vowel is such that it has the first part (เ-), which is always written before the consonant; and the second part (-า) which is always written after the consonant: the consonant to which the vowel belongs is always written between the two (เ-า).

As you progress you will get into the practice of 'reading' (or trying to read, the entire word); and, as there are a few vowels which use เ- as part of their make-up, you will automatically know that the next symbol has to be a consonant and whatever follows, or is written above the consonant will determine what the actual vowel is.

The first consonant is ท, which makes the **/t/** as in *typist* sound wherever it is positioned. The second syllable/word has สระ เ- and **Low Class** ร (/r/ as in *rabbit nibbling*); both consonants in this two-syllable word are initial consonants, and we get **/t/** and **/r/** respectively. This gives us:

/t/ + /ao/ + /r/ + /ai/ = /**tao-rai**/

- HDL
- HLR
- MDL
- MLM
- LDSH
- LDLF
- LLM

Tone Rules

- Syllable 1: **Low Class** + Mái èek = *falling tone*

- Syllable 2: **Low Class** + **Live** syllable = *mid tone* (**LLM**)

เท่าไร = tâo-rai *(how much or how many)*

Example 10 – อะไร

In our next 2-syllable example, we see we have Middle Class อ อ่าง at the beginning of the word; and, from the section on Shortening Vowels, we know that though สระ -ะ is used to shorten certain vowels, this isn't one of them.

So, what is อ doing here? Is it a preceding consonant or a vowel placement consonant?

Here, อ is acting in its vowel placement role, which means we just pronounce the vowel sound.

Note: *it may seem possible that อ could be acting in its preceding consonant role here but you must remember that there are only 4 words in the Thai language in which it performs this function; and, this isn't one of them. Refer to Appendix F - Silent อ*

Our second syllable is the same one we encountered in the previous example:

/**silent**/ + /a/ + /r/ + /ai/ = /<u>a</u>-rai/

Simple Vowels

Tone Rules

- Syllable 1: **M**iddle Class + **D**ead syllable = *low tone* (**MDL**)
- Syllable 2: **L**ow Class + **L**ive syllable = *mid tone* (**LLM**)

อะไร = à-rai (which means *what*)

Example 11 - ไปรษณีย์

In our last example in this section, we have a bit of a mixture. We can see two written vowels (สระ ไ- and สระ ◌ี), 5 consonants, and a punctuation mark over the last consonant.

Consonant Clusters

always begin with

ก, ข, ค, ต, ป, ผ, or พ

*The second consonant is **always***

ร, ล, or ว

If we start at the beginning, we see **Middle Class** consonant ป (/**bp**/ as in **b**ottom **p**it). We've encountered this combination already before, but just to reiterate, when you see this particular consonant, it always pays to look at the next symbol as ป can form consonant clusters. As it transpires, the next consonant, **Low Class** ร (/**r**/ as in **r**abbit **n**ibbling), is a consonant that ป can form clusters with; and, this is exactly what is happening here. Both consonants are initial consonants (/**bp**/ and /**r**/). Putting them together with the vowel, we get:

/bpr/ + /ai/ = /bprai/

Looking at the next consonant, it is **High Class** ษ.

As we have just worked out the first syllable, we know this has to be the initial consonant of the next syllable/word; and, when ษ is in this position, it makes the /**s**/ as in **s**ea **t**rip sound. We must now identify the vowel. As we can't see a written vowel, it has to be unwritten. However, before we can come to this conclusion, we must look at other clues to see if they can assist.

The best way is to look at the next syllable or the end of the word and then work back.

Accordingly, the next written character, and the first consonant in this syllable, is **Low Class** ณ, which makes the /**n**/ as in *Napoleon* sound. It has long vowel สระ ◌ี (/**ii**/ as in *steeple*) written above it.

Is the unwritten vowel between two consonants in the same syllable?

Rule 8

*Unwritten /a/ occurs between 2 consonants in **different syllables**.*

Well, as we've just established that as ณ has a vowel written above it, it must belong to its own syllable (or word, if it's a single syllable word); therefore, the unwritten vowel here must be **between two consonants in different syllables** (/a/). Our second syllable is:

$$/s/ + /a/ = /sa/$$

We've practically covered the last syllable (ณีย์), but what about the last consonant ย์, what's that written above it?

The Gaa-ran

การันต์

The Gaa-ran (◌์)

makes the consonant below it silent.

Well, it's called the *gaa-ran* - การันต์ (◌์), and its purpose is to make the consonant below it silent – it doesn't affect tone calculations. It is commonly used with words that are imported into Thai and can help when spelling or translating Thai-to-imported words.

For example, the popular name *John*, would be written as it is pronounced: **jon**. In Thai, we would write this as จอน. However, from this spelling it could actually be Jon as opposed to John, or even short for Jonathan or Jonathan; we have no way of knowing, it's guesswork.

For some people, the incorrect spelling of their name can be upsetting; and, of course, if you can get it right it makes perfect sense to do so. This is one common use of the *gaa-ran* and is frequently seen in imported words or those adopted from foreign languages in an attempt to keep the spelling close to the original. So, for John, we can use the *gaa-ran* and write จอห์น to clearly distinguish it from Jon.

Another example is with Russ's surname - Crowley. This is spelt เคราลีย์ and again, you can see another use of the gaa-ran at the end.

Example (continued)

Back to our example, from our point of view the consonant makes no sound and does not affect tone or punctuation in any way at all:

$$/n/ + /ii/ = /nii/$$

Putting it all together, we get:

$$/bprai/-/sa/-/nii/$$

- HDL
- HLR
- MDL
- MLM
- LDSH
- LDLF
- LLM

Tone Rules

- Syllable 1: **M**iddle Class + **L**ive syllable = *mid tone* (**MLM**)

- Syllable 2: **H**igh Class + **D**ead syllable = *low tone* (**HDL**)

- Syllable 3: **L**ow Class + **L**ive syllable = *mid tone* (**LLM**)

ไปรษณีย์ = brai-sà-nii (*post office*)

Note: *we hope you're getting used to our system now, in the following chapter we will start introducing some sample sentences and a little grammar so that you can see how it all comes together.*

Please read our section on Reading Strategies in "Reading Strategies" on page 303.

Exercise 8

Exercise 8a

Answers begin on page 345

Match the words to their meaning:

1.	ไหม	to climb	a.
2.	เท่าไร	big, large	b.
3.	ไข่	no, not	c.
4.	ไม่	what	d.
5.	ไปรษณีย์	to use	e.
6.	ใต้	chicken	f.
7.	ได้	how much, how many	g.
8.	ใคร	to give, to let	h.
9.	ไต่	south, underneath	i.
10.	ใส่	egg	j.
11.	ให้	can, be able to (n); to get, to receive (v)	k.
12.	ใหญ่	who	l.
13.	ไก่	a question word, which turns a statement into a question	m.
14.	ใช้	to put in	n
15.	อะไร	post office	o

Exercise 8b

Identify the syllables in these words (draw a vertical line, underline, or highlight the syllables):

1. กำไร	4. เสียใจ	7. ไล่ล่า
2. ภายใน	5. ไปจาก	8. ใยแก้ว
3. เมื่อไร	6. ตอนใต้	9. ในใจ

Their meaning:

1. กำไร – *profit, gain*

2. ภายใน – *inside, interior*

3. เมื่อไร – *when*

4. เสียใจ – *sorry*

5. ไปจาก – *from, to depart, to leave, to go away from*

6. ตอนใต้ – *southern part, south*

7. ไล่ล่า – *to hunt*

8. ใยแก้ว – *fibre glass*

9. ในใจ – *in one's heart, in one's mind.*

สระ เ-า

Next, we're going to look at สระ เ-า. This vowel makes the /**ao**/ as in *mouse* sound and is a long vowel for tone rule purposes.

How is it used?

สระ เ-า is comprised of two vowels that we have already covered and which you should know the respective rules for. Singularly, these rules do not differ here, it's just whenever you see สระ เ-, try and get in the habit of looking to see if there is another vowel above, or immediately after the initial consonant

If there is another vowel, and it is สระ -า, then we have to look at the consonant(s) to see if the vowel is สระ เ-า or something else. If there is just a <u>single consonant</u> then the vowels always combine to form สระ เ-า. If there are <u>two consonants</u> then you need to identify whether these form a consonant cluster or not.

If the consonants do form a consonant cluster, then they are considered a single consonant and the vowel is สระ เ-า; if the consonants don't form a consonant cluster, then สระ เ- and สระ -า are separate vowels and make their own separate sounds (/**ee**/ and /**aa**/ respectively).

For example, we have two words: เวลา and เปล่า.

In the first word, Table 3 (page 16) shows us that ว is never an initial consonant in a consonant cluster, so we know the 2 consonants (ว and ล) and the 2 vowels (สระ เ- and สระ -า) are separate (เว-ลา). We look this word up in our dictionary, and see it is:

$$/w/ + /ee/ + /l/ + /aa/ = /wee/ - /laa/$$

- HDL
- HLR
- MDL
- MLM
- LDSH
- LDLF
- LLM

Tone Rules

Syllable 1: Low Class + Live syllable = *mid tone* (**LLM**)

Syllable 2: Low Class + Live syllable = *mid tone* (**LLM**)

เวลา = wee-laa (*time*)

Consonant Clusters
begin with
ก, ข, ค, ต,
ป, ผ, *or* พ.
The second consonant is **always**
ร, ล, *or* ว.

However, in the second word, Table 3 shows us that ป can be an initial consonant in a cluster. We then look at the second consonant to see if it is a consonant that ป can form clusters with: Table 4 shows us that ร and ล can form clusters with ป. This is what is happening here and, as there is a consonant cluster, they are considered a single consonant (/ปล/) and the vowel is สระ เ-า.

Tone Mark

Middle Class + Mái èek = *low tone*

เปล่า = bplào (*not*, or *empty, blank, vacant*)

One Syllable Words

We'll now look at some single syllable words that use สระ เ-า:

- เมา
- เก่า
- เช้า
- เก้า
- เขา
- เข้า

Example 1 – เมา

In example 1, we see the **Low Class** consonant ม (/**m**/ as in **m**ap) and สระ เ-า. Together, this gives us:

$$/m/ + /ao/ = /mao/$$

Tone Rules

Low Class + Live syllable = **m**id tone (**LLM**)

เมา = mao (drunk)

<u>Sample Sentence</u>

ผู้ชายคนนั้นเมา

- ผู้ชาย – man
- คน – classifier for a person
- นั้น – that
- เมา – drunk

Man [classifier] that drunk

or

That man is drunk

Grammar

Thai uses a similar sentence structure to English:

subject + verb + object

เป็น

is <u>never</u> followed by an adjective.

Here, the subject is ผู้ชายคนนั้น, the verb is เป็น, and the object is เมา; but, in Thai, you don't voice the verb in front of an adjective, therefore the sentence is ผู้ชายคนนั้นเมา.

With the exception of monks and royalty, who use รูป and องค์ respectively, the classifier for people is คน (kon).

The subject here is actually a noun phrase and the form used is:

Noun + classifier + determiner

In our sentence, you see:

ผู้ชายคนนั้นเมา

ผู้ชาย + คน + นั้น

Classifiers

อัน /an/ is the catch-all classifier for things if you don't know the proper one.

Thai uses classifiers with both countable and uncountable nouns (and there are a lot of classifiers in Thai); I haven't come up with an easy way to remember them and you just have to learn these as you go. If you either cannot remember, or simply do not know, the correct classifier, the 'catch-all' classifier for things is อัน (/**an**/). อัน is actually the classifier for **small objects** (which are *things*), but, when all else fails, it will suffice.

Example 2 – เก่า

We now have **Middle Class** consonant ก (/g/ as in *g*alahad *k*night) plus Mái èek:

$$/g/ + /ao/ = /gao/$$

Tone Marks

Middle Class + Mái èek = *low tone*

เก่า = gào *(to be old)*

Sample Sentence

รถยนต์คันนั้นเก่า

- รถยนต์ - *car*
- คัน - classifier for vehicles
- นั้น - *that*

Grammar

This sentence uses the same **subject + verb + object** structure as before: the noun is *car* (รถยนต์), the classifier for vehicles (and spoons and forks) comes next (คัน), followed by the determiner (นั้น), and lastly the adjective (เก่า).

Car [classifier] over there old

The car over there is old.

Example 3 – เก้า

Here we see the tone mark has changed.

Tone Marks

Middle Class + Mái too = *falling tone*

เก้า = gâo ([the number] *nine, 9*)

<u>*Sample Sentence*</u>

ผมมีนัดตอนเก้าโมง

- โมง – hour, o'clock

I have an appointment at nine o'clock in the morning.

Example 4 – เช้า

In this example we have **Low Class** ช (/**ch**/ as in *ch*ef *t*asting):

/**ch**/ + /**ao**/ = / **chao**/

Tone Mark

Low Class + Mái too = *high tone*

เช้า = cháo (*morning*)

<u>*Sample Sentence*</u>

ผมจะไปตลาดตอนเช้า

- ตลาด – *market*

- ตอนเช้า – *morning*

I will go to the market in the morning

Example 5 – เขา

Now we have **High Class** ข (/**k**/ as in *k*angaroo) with no tone mark.

- HDL
- HLR
- MDL
- MLM
- LDSH
- LDLF
- LLM

Tone Rules

High Class + Live syllable = *rising tone* (**HLR**)

เขา= kǎo (it is a personal pronoun which means *he*, *she*, *him*, *her*)

เขา is gender-neutral, as is คุณ (kun), which means *you*, *Mr*, *Mrs*, *Miss*, etc.

Sample Sentence

เขาสวย

- สวย – *beautiful, pretty*

He/she is beautiful.

เป็น

is <u>never</u> followed by an adjective in Thai.

In English, we frequently use the verb *to be*, Thai is different. In English we would say, "*He is good looking", or 'She is pretty'"* and so forth; but, in Thai, though you may be tempted to insert เป็น, it is only used when followed by a noun or a noun phrase, and is <u>never followed by an adjective</u> (*Smyth, 2002, p. 56*). สวย is an adjective.

You could also emphasise this by adding มาก, which is an adverb meaning *very much, a lot;* and, it is used to modify the adjective (**adjective + modifier**):

เขาสวยมาก

She is very beautiful.

You could even over-emphasise by repeating the adverb (remember, in Thai Mái Yá-mók (ๆ) means repeat the previous word - *reduplication*):

เขาสวยมากๆ

He is very, very beautiful.

Note: *you will occasionally see the modifier before the adjective (modifier + adjective). This is mainly with negative sentences but is less common than* **adjective + modifier**.

Example 6 – เข้า

In example 6, we add the tone mark Mái too.

Tone Mark

High Class + Mái too = *falling tone*

เข้า = kâo (*to enter, to get into*)

Sample Sentence

เขาเข้าไปในอาคารนี้

- ไป – *to go*
- ใน – *in*
- อาคาร – *building*
- นี้ – *this*

He/she enter go in building this

or

He entered this building.

Two Syllables/Words

- เก้าอี้
- เท่าไร
- ภูเขา
- เข้าใจ

Example 7 – เก้าอี้

Vowels and Tone Marks
are always written above the initial consonant (except in a cluster, when it's the second consonant).

We can clearly see two syllable/words here. We have already encountered the first syllable/word; but, even if this were not the case, at the end of the word we can see a vowel that is always written above a consonant. This vowel is สระ ◌ี and it makes the /**ii**/ as in *steeple* sound.

Here, we see it written above **Middle Class** อ (/ɔɔ/ as in *awful weather*). If you recall, this consonant can also act as a preceding consonant so we need to work out what the function of อ is here: is it a preceding or is it a vowel placement consonant?

Remember, there are only 4 words in Thai where อ acts as a preceding consonant and this isn't one of them; thus, อ has to be acting as a vowel placement consonant:

/gâo/ + /**silent**/ + /**ii**/ = / gâo/-/ii/

Tone Marks

We already know the first syllable is falling tone, the second syllable has a tone mark:

Middle Class + Mái too = *falling tone*

เก้าอี้ = gâo-ĩ (*chair*)

ผมนั่งบนเก้าอี้

- นั่ง – _to sit_

- บน – _on_

I sat on the chair.

Example 8 – เท่าไร

We have encountered this word before, it is a question word which means _how much,_ or _how many_.

Tone Rules

- HDL
- HLR
- MDL
- MLM
- LDSH
- LDLF
- LLM

We have one syllable with a tone mark, and one without; so the tone for this example is:

- Syllable 1: **Low Class + Mái èek** = _falling tone_

- Syllable 2: **Low Class + Live syllable** = _**m**id tone_ (**LLM**)

เท่าไร = tâo-rai _(how much or how many)_

Sample Sentence

นี่ราคาเท่าไร

- นี่ – _this_

- (ราคา) เท่าไร – _how much_

How much is this?

Note: ราคา _means price and the brackets indicate this is optional when it is obvious that you are referring to the price of something, e.g. you are holding or pointing at a specific object._

Example 9 – ภูเขา

In Thai, there are only two vowels that are written underneath a consonant, one is short, and the other long. Here we see the long vowel สระ ◌ู, which makes the /**uu**/ as in *boot* sound, written underneath **Low Class** ภ, which always makes the /**p**/ as in *painting* sound. We know this second syllable and together this gives us:

/**p**/ + /**uu**/ + /**k**/ + /**ao**/ = /**puu**/-/**kao**/

Tone Rules

- Low Class + Live syllable = *m*id tone (**LLM**)
- High Class + Live syllable = *r*ising tone (**HLR**)

ภูเขา = puu-kǎo (*hill* or *mountain*)

Sample Sentence

จอห์นต้องการปีนภูเขาลูกนั้น

- จอห์น – *John*

- ต้องการ – *to want*

- ปีน – *to climb*

- ลูก – classifier for hills, mountains, hurricanes, storms and anything small and round, such as fruit, balls.
- นั้น – *that*

John want climb mountain [classifier] that

or

John wants to climb that mountain.

Example 10 – เข้าใจ

You know all the shapes and sounds in this last example and we can move straight to the sounds:

/k/ + /ao/ + /j/ + /ai/ = /kao/ - /jai/

- HDL
- HLR
- MDL
- MLM
- LDSH
- LDLF
- LLM

Tone Rules

- High Class + Mái too = *falling tone*

- **M**iddle Class + **L**ive syllable = *mid tone* (**MLM**)

เข้าใจ = kâo-jai (*to understand*)

Sample Sentence

ดิฉันเข้าใจ

- ดิฉัน = personal pronoun (for a female)

I understand.

or, if we want to negate the sentence, we just add ไม่:

ดิฉัน**ไม่**เข้าใจ

I do not understand.

Exercise 9

Exercise 9a

Answers begin on page 345

Match the words to their meaning:

1.	เช้า	beautiful, pretty	a.
2.	นั้น	man	b.
3.	เมา	9	c.
4.	คัน	that	d.
5.	ตลาด	classifier for person	e.
6.	เข้า	building	f.
7.	เขา	not, or empty, blank, vacant	g.
8.	รถยนต์	chair	h.
9.	เก้าอี้	to enter, to go into	i.
10.	อาคาร	classifier for vehicles	j.
11.	เก้า	morning	k.
12.	สวย	he, she, him, her	l.
13.	เปล่า	drunk	m.
14.	คน	market	n
15.	ผู้ชาย	car	o

Exercise 9b

Identify the syllables in these words (draw a vertical line, underline, or highlight the syllables):

1. เท่าไร   4. เช้ามืด   7. เก่าแก

2. เกาหลี   5. เข้ามา   8. เช่าซื้อ

3. เก้าแสน   6. เงามืด   9. เช้าวันน

Their meaning:

1. เท่าไร - *how much*

2. เกาหลี - *Korean*

3. เก้าแสน - *900,000*

4. เช้ามืด - *dawn, daybreak, sunrise*

5. เข้ามา - *to enter, to get in*

6. เงามืด - *shadow, shade*

7. เก่าแก่ - *ancient, old*

8. เช่าซื้อ - *to hire purchase, to rent by installment*

9. เช้าวันนี้ - *this morning.*

Notes

สระ ◌ิ and สระ ◌ี

By now, you should be used to the format for these sections and are hopefully getting a good feel for how things progress. We also hope that you now realise that reading Thai isn't all that difficult and once you have structure and a process it just requires practice - the same as any other skill. We are now going to change tack and move things along by looking at vowels in pairs.

In this post we will look at สระ ◌ิ and สระ ◌ี. We have encountered these vowels before in our examples and you should recognise or remember that these make the /i/ as in *lip* and the /ii/ as in *steeple* sounds, respectively.

How are they used?

As we know, unless there is a consonant cluster, vowels written above a consonant are always written above the initial consonant. Again, this is a great indicator to help us identify where a word or syllable begins. If there is a consonant cluster, then the vowel is written above the second consonant; and, as a cluster is considered a single consonant, the rule is still applicable.

One Syllable Words

- คิด
- ดิบ
- ดี
- กี่

- นิ̀

- ขิ̀

- สิ̄

Example 1 - คิด

In the first example, we see we have the short vowel สระ ◌̂ written above the initial consonant **Low Class** ค (/**k**/ as in **k**oala). We also see that the final consonant is **Middle Class** ด (/**t**/ as in **d**amsel **t**ower) and together they give us:

$$/\text{k}/ + /i/ + /t/ = /\text{kit}/$$

- HDL
- HLR
- MDL
- MLM
- LDSH
- LDLF
- LLM

Tone Rules

Low Class + **D**ead syllable and **SH**ort vowel = *high tone* (**LDSH**)

คิด = kit (*to think, to consider, to calculate, to charge a price*)

Sample Sentence

ผมจะคิดดูนะ

- คิดดู – on its own, คิด means *to think*, but when used with ดู it means *you are considering or thinking about something.*

- นะ – a particle used to make a sentence seem less abrupt, softer even.

I will think about it.

Example 2 – ดิบ

For our next example using the short vowel, we have **Middle Class** ด in the

initial consonant position (/**d**/ as in **d**amsel **t**ower), then our short vowel สระ

◌ิ, and **Middle Class** บ as the final consonant (/**p**/ as in **b**ald **p**atch):

$$/d/ + /i/ + /p/ = /dip/$$

Tone Rules

Middle Class + **D**ead syllable = *low tone* (**MDL**)

ดิบ = dìp *(uncooked, raw)*

<u>Sample Sentence</u>

ผมไม่กินอาหารดิบ

- อาหาร – *food*

I don't eat raw food.

Example 3 – ดี

In this example we see just a single consonant, **Middle Class** ด (/**d**/ as in

damsel **t**ower), and long vowel สระ ◌ี (/**ii**/ as in *st**ee**ple*):

$$/d/ + /ii/ = /dii/$$

Tone Rules

Middle Class + **L**ive syllable = *mid tone* (**MLM**)

ดี = dii *(good)*

Sample Sentence

เขาเป็นคนดี

He is a good man.

Example 4 – กี่

Staying with this theme (there are many common words using this simple form), we now have **Middle Class** ก (/**g**/ as in **g**alahad **k**night), and long vowel สระ ี.

$$/g/ + /ii/ = /gii/$$

Tone Mark

Middle Class + Mái èek = _low tone_

กี่ = gïi (how many)

Sample Sentence

คุณมีบ้านกี่หลัง

กี่

is always followed by a classifier of the item being counted.

- บ้าน – _house, home_

- หลัง – classifier for a house

How many houses do you have?

Example 5 – นี่

We have **Low Class** น as the initial consonant (/**n**/ as in **n**avigating), and the tone mark Mái èek:

$$/n/ + /ii/ = /nii/$$

Tone Mark

Low Class + Mái èek = *falling tone*

นี่ = nîi (*this*)

<u>*Sample Sentence*</u>

นี่ราคาเท่าไร

How much is this?

Example 6 – ขี่

Here we just change the initial consonant to **High Class** ข (/**k**/ as in **k**anga-roo):

/**k**/ + /**ii**/ = /**kii**/

Tone Mark

High Class + Mái èek = *low tone*

ขี่ = kìi *(to ride)*

<u>*Sample Sentence*</u>

เขาชอบขี่รถจักรยาน

- ชอบ – *to like*

- รถจักรยาน – *bicycle*

She likes riding a bicycle.

Remember, เขา is gender neutral so it could equally be *He likes riding a bicycle.* Of course, if the subject is unclear you would use their name instead, but this example just illustrates usage.

Example 7 – สี

In our final single syllable word example, we have **High Class** ส (/**s**/ as in **s**quirrel **t**ail) and the long vowel:

$$/s/ + /ii/ = /sii/$$

- HDL
- HLR
- MDL
- MLM
- LDSH
- LDLF
- LLM

Tone Rules

High Class + **Live** syllable = *rising tone* (**HLR**)

 สี = sǐi (it means *colour*)

Colours

- สีดำ (sǐi-dam) – *black*

- สีแดง (sǐi-dɛɛng) – *red*

- สีน้ำเงิน (sǐi-nám-ngəən) – *dark blue*

- สีฟ้า (sǐi-fáa) – *light blue*

- สีขาว (sǐi-kǎao) – *white*

- สีเหลือง (sǐi-lɨɨang) – *yellow*

Sample Sentence

รถยนต์คันนั้นสีแดง

That car is red.

Two Syllables/Words

- ติดกับ

- คิดว่า

- ดีมาก

- กีฬา

Example 8 – ติดกับ

We can see two vowels in this example. The first one is the vowel we are looking at in this section, which is always written above an initial consonant. The second vowel is a medial vowel and is always written between two consonants (we covered this in "สระ -ะ & อ-" on page 67). These characteristics make it easy to recognise both syllables/words.

A quick glance tells us that all these consonants are all **Middle Class**. However, please remember that the first consonant (ต) makes the /**dt**/ as in *dam-sel tower* sound as an initial consonant, and the second consonant (ด) makes the /**t**/ as in *damsel tower* sound when it is in the terminal position.

For the second syllable/word, we have 2 consonants that we are familiar with: /**g**/ as in *galahad knight* and /**p**/ as in *bald patch*:

$$/\textbf{dt}/ + /\textbf{i}/ + /\textbf{t}/ - /\textbf{g}/ + /\textbf{a}/ + /\textbf{p}/ = /\textbf{dtit}/-/\textbf{gap}/$$

Tone Rules

- Syllable 1: **M**iddle Class + **D**ead syllable = *low tone* (**MDL**)
- Syllable 2: **M**iddle Class + **D**ead syllable = *low tone* (**MDL**)

ติดกับ = dtìt-gàp *(to adjoin, to connect, to trap, close to)*

บ้านของฉันอยู่ติดกับสวนสาธารณะ

- ของ – *of, belonging to, things, possessions.* Here, we say *'house of mine'*.

- สวน – *garden, park, field*

- สวนสาธารณะ – *public park*

My house is close to the park.

Example 9 – คิดว่า

Next, we see one short vowel in the first syllable/word, and a long vowel in the second. The first syllable/word is a slight variation on the previous example, as we now have **Low Class** consonant ค as the initial consonant (/**k**/ as in **k**oala). The second syllable/word is comprised of **Low Class** ว (/**w**/ as in **w**ave **o**ver), Mái èek, and สระ –า. This gives us:

/k/ + /i/ + /t/ - /w/ + /aa/ = /kít/-/wâa/

Tone Rules

- Syllable 1: **L**ow Class + **D**ead syllable and **Sh**ort vowel = *high tone* (**LDSH**)

- Syllable 2: Low Class + Mái èek = *falling tone*

คิดว่า = kít-wâa (to show or express an idea
about something: 'think that...')

ผมคิดว่าเราควรไปทะเลนะ

- ควร – kuan (*should, ought to.* We haven't covered the use of the vowel used here but will do so in "สระ -วั๊ะ and สระ -วั๊" on page 279; however, you should be familiar with the sound).

- ทะเล = *sea, ocean*

  I think we should go to the sea.

Example 10 – ดีมาก

Here we see the long vowel above the initial **Middle Class** consonant ด (/**d**/ as in **d**amsel **t**ower). We also see สระ -า between **Low Class** ม (/**m**/ as in **m**ap), and **Middle Class** ก (/**k**/ as in **g**alahad **k**night).

We know that สระ -า is always written after a consonant in the <u>same sylla-ble</u>, so this obviously means that ม is the initial consonant of the second syllable/word. We now have:

$$/\textbf{d}/ + /\textbf{ii}/ - /\textbf{m}/ + /\textbf{aa}/ + /\textbf{k}/ = /\textbf{dii}/\text{-}/\textbf{maak}/$$

Tone Rules

- Syllable 1: **M**iddle Class + **L**ive syllable = *mid tone* (**MLM**)
- Syllable 2: **L**ow Class + **D**ead syllable and **L**ong vowel = *falling tone* (**LDLF**)

  ดีมาก = dii-mâak *(very good)*

Sample Sentence

หนังเรื่องนี้ดีมาก

- หนัง – *movie, film*

- เรื่อง – rûuang (it is a classifier for a movie. Alternative meanings, in different contexts, are: *about, regarding, concerning.* This word uses a vowel we haven't covered as yet; we will cover it later in the book).

This movie is very good.

Example 11 – กีฬา

Again, we identify the vowels and see the same two as used in the previous example and neither syllable/word has a terminal consonant. I won't repeat what the initial consonant of the 1st syllable is as you should be very familiar with it now and it has the long vowel written above it. The second syllable consists of **Low Class** ฬ, which makes the /l/ as in *look nice* sound when an initial consonant, plus สระ -า as the written vowel:

/g/ + /ii/ + /l/ + /aa/ = /gii/-/laa/

Tone Rules

- Syllable 1: **M**iddle Class + **L**ive syllable = *mid tone* (**MLM**)
- Syllable 2: **L**ow Class + **L**ive syllable = *mid tone* (**LLM**)

กีฬา = gii-laa *(sport)*

<u>Sample Sentence</u>

พวกเราชอบเล่นกีฬา

- พวกเรา – *we, us*
- เล่น – *to play*

We like playing sports.

Exercise 10

Exercise 10a

Answers begin on page 345

Match the words to their meaning:

1.	นี่	black	a.	
2.	ดี	how many	b.	
3.	ของ	uncooked, raw	c.	
4.	คิด	to like	d.	
5.	ทะเล	to think, to consider, to calculate, to charge a price	e.	
6.	ขี่	this	f.	
7.	สีดำ	very good	g.	
8.	กี่	to ride	h.	
9.	เล่น	indicates possession, belonging to, things	i.	
10.	ดิบ	house	j.	
11.	ดีมาก	food	k.	
12.	อาหาร	sea, ocean	l.	
13.	บ้าน	garden, park, field	m.	
14.	สวน	to play	n	
15.	ชอบ	good	o	

Exercise 10b

Identify the syllables in these words (don't forget unwritten vowels):

1. กิริยา	4. ญี่ปุ่น	7. กิเลส
2. คดี	5. ตัดสิน	8. นาฬิกา
3. ชีวิต	6. นิยม	9. พิพิธภัณฑ์

Their meaning:

1. กิริยา - *action, manners, behaviour, conduct*

2. คดี - *lawsuit, legal action, case*

3. ชีวิต - *life*

4. ญี่ปุ่น - *Japan*

5. ตัดสิน - *referee, judge, decide*

6. นิยม - *popular*

7. กิเลส - *lust, evil wish, greed, desire*

8. นาฬิกา - *clock, watch, timepiece*

9. พิพิธภัณฑ์ - museum.

Notes

สระ◌ุ and สระ◌ู

We have encountered both these vowels in words we've already used and in this section we'll look at what makes สระ◌ุ and สระ◌ู unique.

How are they used?

สระ◌ุ and สระ◌ู are the only two characters in the Thai alphabet that are written underneath consonants; they make the **/u/** as in *crook,* and the **/uu/** as in *boot* sounds, respectively.

In a similar way to vowels that are written above consonants, สระ◌ุ and สระ◌ู are always found beneath the initial consonant in a syllable or a word. Again, this is yet another clue that helps us to break down sentences and to identify where syllables and words begin and end. Remember, a consonant cluster is considered a single consonant, so when you see either of these vowels written underneath the second consonant in a syllable or a word then the consonants must either form a consonant cluster or the consonants will be in separate syllables and there will be an unwritten vowel (/**a**/) between them.

For example, if you see the word สรุป then we need to know if ส forms consonant clusters. Table 4 on page 17 shows us that it doesn't and, as they are in different syllables, we now know there must be an unwritten /**a**/ between ส and ร.

สรุป = sà-rùp *(to sum up, or conclude)*

Note: If you're thinking the second syllable should be *high tone*, refer to Appendix E - Preceding Consonants.

However, if we see a word such as กรุง (and if you are in Bangkok, you see this all the time), then we know that ก and ร do form consonant clusters and the vowel is, to all intents and purposes, beneath the first, clustered consonant: กรุง (grung) means *capital city*, *city* or *town*.

One Syllable Words

- กู้
- คลุม
- พุทธ
- ครู
- งู

- ดู
- พูด
- รู้
- รูป

Example 1 – กู้

In our first example, we have **Middle Class** ก, tone mark Mái too, and long vowel สระ ◌ู:

- HDL
- HLR
- MDL
- MLM
- LDSH
- LDLF
- LLM

$$/g/ + /uu/ = /guu/$$

Tone Mark

Middle Class + Mái too = *falling tone*

กู้ = gûu (*to borrow [money, with interest]*; or, *to salvage a ship*; or, *to save face in a situation*)

Sample Sentence

ผมขอกู้เงินหน่อยได้ไหม

- ขอ...ได้ไหม – *may*

- เงิน – *money, cash*

- หน่อย – it can mean a *little*, *a little bit*; or, it can be used to soften a request (making it more polite).

May I borrow some money?

With ขอ...ได้ไหม, the ellipsis means both parts of this phrase are used and what is written or spoken between the parts is what the request specifically refers to.

Example 2 - คลุม

As this is a single word example, it is easy to spot that this is a consonant cluster. We have **Low Class** consonants ค and ล forming the cluster (/k/ as in *k*oala, and /l/ as in *l*arge *n*ugget), our short vowel, and **Low Class** ม in the final position (/m/ as in *m*ap):

/kl/ + /u/ + /m/ = /klum/

Tone Rules

Low Class + Live syllable = *mid tone* (**LLM**)

คลุม = klum (*to cover, unclear, enveloped*)

Sample Sentence

อย่าลืมคลุมเตียงด้วยนะ

- อย่า – *do not, don't, never*

- ลืม – *to forget*

- เตียง – *bed*

- ด้วย – *also, as well*

- นะ – a polite particle used in requests.

Don't forget to cover your bed.

Example 3 - พุทธ

We have three **Low Class** consonants and the short vowel in this example. We haven't encountered this kind of syllable/word-ending combination before, but you would be forgiven for thinking there is an unwritten vowel between the second and third consonant; however, there isn't.

The consonants are พ (/**p**/ as in **p**raying), ท (/**t**/ as in **t**ypist), and ธ (/**t**/ as in **t**eabag).

This word is a borrowed word from Sanskrit and the rules are slightly different here. There aren't too many borrowed words, so the best thing to do is to be aware they exist and then learn them as they arise. Furthermore, this is another reason why a good dictionary is essential and why you need to remember words and their characteristics. We have:

$$/p/ + /u/ + /t/ + /t/ = /putt/$$

Phonetically, it serves no purpose to have a double-t at the end of this word. Another reason is you may think of incorrectly pronouncing this word as if you were standing on the green and about to take a golf stroke. So, removing the second /t/ we have:

$$/put/$$

Tone Rules

Low Class + Dead syllable and Short vowel = *high tone* (**LDSH**)

พุทธ = pút (*Buddha*)

Sample Sentence

ฉันสวดมนต์ต่อหน้าพระพุทธรูปทุกวัน

- สวดมนต์ – *to pray*

- ต่อหน้า – *in front of, before*

- พระพุทธ – *Lord Buddha, Buddha*

- พระพุทธรูป – *image of Buddha*

    I pray in front of the image of Buddha every day.

Note: *hopefully you get the idea of our system now. From hereon, we won't bold the text everytime we say Low, Middle or High Class consonant.*

Note: when there is a word after พุทธ, unwritten vowel **/a/** is inserted after ธ. For example, พุทธศาสนา (pút-tá-sàat-sà-nǎa) - *Buddhism.*

Example 4 – ครู

In this example, we're moving onto the long vowel. Bearing in mind the rule about consonant clusters and it's plain there is one here.

We have Low Class consonants ค and ร in the initial position, plus สระ ◌ู:

/**kr**/ + /**uu**/ = /**kruu**/

Tone Rules

Low Class + Live syllable = *mid tone* (**LLM**)

ครู = kruu *(teacher, instructor)*

<u>*Sample Sentence*</u>

ผมชอบครูภาษาไทยของผม

I like my Thai teacher.

Example 5 - งู

An easy example here, with Low Class ง (**/ng/** as in *guardi**ng***)*, and the long version of the vowel:

/ng/ + /uu/ = /nguu/

- HDL
- HLR
- MDL
- MLM
- LDSH
- LDLF
- LLM

Tone Rules

Low Class + Live syllable = *mid tone* (**LLM**)

งู = nguu *(snake)*

- ง งู – the seventh letter of the Thai alphabet.

<u>*Sample Sentence*</u>

ฉันไม่ชอบงู

I don't like snakes.

Example 6 – ดู

Here, we simply swap the consonant and get:

/d/ + /uu/ = /duu/

Tone Rules

Middle Class + Live syllable = *mid tone* (**MLM**)

ดู = duu (*to look at*, *to watch* (e.g. a film), *to examine*)

Sample Sentence

ผมกำลังดูหนัง

I'm watching the movie

Example 7 – พูด

With two consonants in this word, we see the vowel is written under the first consonant. We have Low Class พ as an initial consonant (**/p/** as in *praying*), the long vowel สระ ู, and terminal consonant ด.

/p/ + /uu/ + /t/ = /puut/

- HDL
- HLR
- MDL
- MLM
- LDSH
- LDLF
- LLM

Tone Rules

Low Class + Dead syllable and Long vowel = *falling tone* (**LDLF**)

พูด = pûut (*to speak, to talk, to say*)

Sample Sentence

เขาพูดภาษาไทย

She speaks Thai.

Consonant Names

You should be getting the hang of the consonants now and for the common consonants, instead of writing 'Low Class consonant ค (/**k**/ as in **k**oala)...', we will just write 'Low Class ค';

From my own point of view, I rarely refer to the picture names now; but, as I'm not a native speaker of Thai, it's still not 100% automatic. Occasionally I have to pause and think about the sounds, especially when trying to work them out; yet, though most of the time it's possible to do so, there are occasions when it isn't.

As we saw in example 3 (พุทธ) following any of the stated rules won't help you, you either need a dictionary (พจนานุกรม) or you have to ask someone.

However, though our system is excellent to help you learn the alphabet, and to get you started reading Thai, it does have its limitations. First of all, once you've mastered the alphabet and start to read, it's important that you take the time and effort to learn the actual consonant and vowel names: you can't spell a word, or have someone spell a word to you unless you know the consonant names (if you try it with our picture names, expect a strange look back).

Second, and in case you glossed over it before, our system and these guides are merely the starting point in your quest: we get you to the point where you know how to understand and read basic Thai; and, from that point, you are then only limited by your own personal aspirations. To take it further will require additional material and effort on your behalf. It isn't easy and it's not necessarily quick, but it is exciting, it is rewarding, and it is fun!

We hope you think and feel the same and if you want to let us know how you're getting on, what you find difficult, easy, or require extra clarification on, then feel free to email me: **russ@learnthaialphabet.com**.

Regards,

Russ

Example 8 – รู้

No difficulties here with Low Class ร and Mái too:

$$/r/ + /uu/ = /ruu/$$

Tone Mark

Low Class + Mái too = *high tone*

รู้ = rúu (*to know* [a subject or piece of learned information])

<u>Sample Sentence</u>

ผมรู้ว่าเขาไม่ใช่คนไทย

- รู้ว่า – *to know that*

- ไม่ใช่ – *[to] be not; no*

> *I know that he is not a Thai.*

Example 9 - รูป

Moving on, we drop the tone mark and add Middle Class ป as the final consonant (/**p**/ as in *bottom **p**it*):

$$/r/ + /uu/ + /p/ = /ruup/$$

- HDL
- HLR
- MDL
- MLM
- LDSH
- LDLF
- LLM

Tone Rules

Low Class + Dead syllable and Long vowel = *falling tone* (**LDLF**)

รูป = rûup (*picture, shape, appearance, form*)

Sample Sentence

ผมจะซื้อรูปนั้น

- ซื้อ - *to buy, to purchase, to pay for*

I will buy that picture.

Note: To fully understand the last example in the following section, you need to have read the section in the Appendix on Preceding Consonants (page 335). Please do that before you continue.

Two Syllables/Words

- กรุงเทพฯ
- รู้จัก
- วันศุกร์
- สนุก

Example 10 - กรุงเทพฯ

Among the consonants we can see two vowels and a punctuation mark at the end. We saw the first part of this word earlier, but if we didn't know this how would we break it down?

The second vowel that we can see is สระ เ- and we know that particular vowel always marks the start of a syllable or word; therefore, we can straightaway see that the second syllable/word is เทพ. Notwithstanding some peculiarity in the language or the spelling, we can confidently predict that the last consonant (พ) is the final consonant of the second syllable/word:

$$/t/ + /ee/ + /p/ = /teep/$$

We know that ก and ร are commonly seen as consonant clusters, if not then there will be an unwritten vowel between them; however, we did look at this word before, so I won't drag it out. Putting them together, we have:

$$/gr/ + /u/ + /ng/ = /grung/-/teep/$$

Before we look at the punctuation we will calculate the tone.

- HDL
- HLR
- MDL
- MLM
- LDSH
- LDLF
- LLM

Tone Rules

- Syllable 1: **M**iddle Class + **L**ive syllable = *mid tone* (**MLM**)
- Syllable 2: **L**ow Class + **D**ead syllable and **L**ong vowel = *falling tone* (**LDLF**)

กรุงเทพ = grung-têep

Punctuation

ๆ

means abbreviated form. You must always pronounce the full form in formal sittuations (if you know it, of course)

The punctuation mark Bpee-yaan-nɔ́ɔi (ๆ) is used for abbreviations and when you see this you have to pronounce the full term when speaking (if you do actually know it). The day-to-day, full term for กรุงเทพๆ is

กรุงเทพมหานคร (กรุง-เทพ-ม-หา-น-คร); in English, we call it Bangkok, the capital city of Thailand.

กรุงเทพมหานคร is itself a shortened version of the full term:

กรุงเทพมหานคร อมรรัตนโกสินทร์ มหินทรายุธยา มหาดิลกภพ
นพรัตนราชธานีบูรีรมย์ อุดมราชนิเวศน์มหาสถาน
อมรพิมานอวตารสถิต สักกะทัตติยวิษณุกรรมประสิทธิ์

This means:

"The city of angels, the great city, the residence of the Emerald Buddha, the impregnable city (unlike Ayutthaya) of God Indra, the grand capital of the world endowed with nine precious gems, the happy city, abounding in an enormous Royal Palace that resembles the heavenly abode where reigns the reincarnated god, a city given by Indra and built by Vishnukarn." [7]

Sample Sentence

ฉันอาศัยอยู่ที่กรุงเทพฯ

- อาศัย = *to live, to reside, to dwell*

I live in Bangkok.

Example 11 - รู้จัก

Here we can clearly see two written vowels: we have สระ ฺ beneath initial Low Class consonant ร, and we have Mái Hăn-aa-ġaat (อ้-) between Middle Class จ and ก. As Mái Hăn-aa-ġaat is a medial vowel it identifies the initial and final consonant in the second syllable (or word) and easily separates the two parts in this example:

/r/ + /uu/ + /j/ + /a/ + /k/ = /ruu/-/jak/

---

7. http://www.omg-facts.com/History/The-Real-Name-Of-Bangkok-Is-The-Longest/51705

- HDL
- HLR
- MDL
- MLM
- LDSH
- LDLF
- LLM

Tone Rules

- Syllable 1: Low Class + Mái too = *high tone*

- Syllable 2: **M**iddle Class + **D**ead syllable = *low tone* (**MDL**)

รู้จัก = rúu- jàk (*know* (*a person* or *place*)).

Sample Sentence

ผมรู้จักผู้ชายคนนั้น

I know that man.

Example 12 – วันศุกร์

In our next example, we can again see two written vowels. We know short สระ ◌ุ is always written underneath an initial consonant and therefore High Class ศ is the initial consonant of the second syllable (/**s**/ as in **s**ign **t**op).

Mái Hăn-aa-ġaat (◌ั) is written between Low Class consonants ว and น (/**w**/ as in **w**ave **o**ver and /**n**/ as in **n**avigating), and these identify the initial and the final consonants of the first syllable; but, what about the last two conso-

nants, ก and ร, do these form a new syllable/word (with an unwritten vowel between them)?

การันต์

It makes the conso-nant below it silent.

If you remember the name and the purpose of the symbol above ร, it's called the gaa-ran (◌์) and its purpose is to make the consonant beneath it silent. There is no unwritten vowel between this consonant and the consonant before it; so, in this instance, ก is the terminal consonant.

/w/ + /a/ + /n/ + /s/ + /u/ + /k/ + /silent/ = /wan/-/suk/

Simple Vowels 189

Tone Rules

- Syllable 1: **Low Class** + **Live** syllable = *mid tone* (**LLM**)
- Syllable 2: **High Class** + **Dead** syllable = *low tone* (**HDL**)

วันศุกร์ = wan-sùk (it means *Friday*)

<u>Sample Sentence</u>

ฉันมีเรียนภาษาไทยวันศุกร์

- เรียน = *to learn, to study*

I have a Thai class on Friday.

Example 13 - สนุก

Consonant Clusters *begin with*

ก, ข, ค, ต,

ป, ผ, *or* พ.

*The second consonant is **always*** ร, ล, *or* ว.

In the final example in this section, we see the short vowel written beneath the middle of three consonants. Is this a consonant cluster? If you need to, a quick glance at Table 3 on page 16 will show you that neither of the first two consonants is ever found in any consonant cluster.

As สระ ┐ is always written underneath an initial consonant, Low Class น <u>has to be</u> the initial consonant of the second syllable.

This means that High Class ส has to be in a different syllable and there has

Rule 8

*Unwritten /a/ occurs between 2 consonants in **different syllables***.

to be an unwritten vowel between it and น. We already established that น is the initial consonant of the second syllable; therefore (as rule 8 states) the unwritten vowel has to be /a/.

The final consonant of the second syllable is ก, which makes the /k/ sound when it is in the final position:

/s/ + /a/ + /n/ + /u/ + /k/ = /sa/-/<u>n</u>uk/

Tone Rules

- **HDL**
- **HLR**
- **MDL**
- **MLM**
- **LDSH**
- **LDLF**
- **LLM**

- Syllable 1: **H**igh Class + **D**ead syllable = *low tone* (**HDL**)

  When calculating tone, for words starting with a High Class consonant followed by a Low Class consonant **and which are not** consonant clusters, e.g. สนุก, สว่าง, สนาม, etc., you must add [unwritten] ห in front of the second consonant/syllable for calculating tone. This then means the syllable begins with a High Class consonant. This is one of the preceding consonant rules we mentioned earlier (refer to Appendix E - Preceding Consonants).

- Syllable 2: **H**igh Class + **D**ead syllable = *low tone* (**HDL**)

สนุก = sà- nùk (fun, enjoyable, entertaining,
amusing, or pleasant)

<u>*Sample Sentence*</u>

การเรียนภาษาไทยสนุกนะ

Learning Thai is fun.

Exercise 11

Exercise 11a

Answers begin on page 346

Match the words to their meaning:

1.	ครู	to look at, to watch a film	a.	
2.	ดู	picture, shape, appearance, form	b.	
3.	รู้	snake	c.	
4.	พุทธ	to cover, to conceal, to envelop	d.	
5.	สรุป	teacher, instructor	e.	
6.	สนุก	Bangkok	f.	
7.	คลุม	no, not	g.	
8.	เรียน	money, cash	h.	
9.	รูป	Buddha	i.	
10.	วันศุกร์	to learn, to study	j.	
11.	เงิน	Friday	k.	
12.	กรุงเทพ	to sum up, to conclude	l.	
13.	ไม่ใช่	to speak, to talk, to say	m.	
14.	งู	fun	n	
15.	พูด	to know a subject or learned information	o	

Exercise 11b

Identify the syllables in these words (draw a vertical line, underline, or highlight the syllables):

1. วันศุกร์   4. ประตู   7. ครูฝึก

2. รู้สึก   5. ประชุม   8. ดูเหมือน

3. มนุษย์   6. บุหรี่   9. มิถุนายน

Their meaning:

1. วันศุกร์ – *Friday*

2. รู้สึก – *to feel, to emote, to feel an emotion, to experience*

3. มนุษย์ – *human being, man, homo sapien*

4. ประตู – *door, gate*

5. ประชุม – *to assemble, to have a meeting*

6. บุหรี่ – *cigarette*

7. ครูฝึก – *trainer, coach*

8. ดูเหมือน – *to seem like*

9. มิถุนายน – *June.*

สระ ◌ำ and สระ ◌ื

We have already looked at two of the vowels that are always written above an initial consonant in Thai and in this section we will look at the other two: สระ ◌ื and สระ ◌ื.

สระ ◌ื makes the /ʉ/ as in *push-up* sound and สระ ◌ื makes the /ʉʉ/ as in *bloom* sound.

Note: *this sound has no English equivalent, and is perhaps the most difficult to get correct. To get close to making these sounds correctly, when you pronounce the sounds /ʉ/ and /ʉʉ/ your lips stay 'normal', just open them a bit to let the air out. In the previous chapter, you saw the vowels that make the /u/ and the /uu/ sounds; and, with these you round your lips in the same manner as when you whistle to let the air out.*

One effective way to learn is to listen to the sounds in the Learn Thai Alphabet application to see the difference between /u/ and /ʉ/, or /uu/ and /ʉʉ/; however, the best method of all is to get a native Thai speaker to assist you.

How are they used?

As we know, identifying where the vowels are written is the key factor in determining where syllable and word breaks are and these vowels are no exception. As we have seen throughout, we need to distinguish between the long and the short vowel in order to pronounce the syllable or word correctly and also for calculating tone.

Rules for Reading Thai

Casting back to the rules, do you remember rule 6?

We haven't covered it yet in the main body so the chances are you may have forgotten it:

Rule 6
Sà-rà **ʉʉa** (ˉ) is **always** followed
by a final consonant.

What this means is that not all syllables or words will necessarily have a final consonant; and if the word doesn't have one, then a vowel placement consonant is provided. This 'inserted' vowel placement consonant is อ อ่าง and, in this capacity, it is always silent.

One Syllable Words

- นึ่ง
- ดึง
- คือ
- ผึ้ง

- ซื้อ
- หรือ
- ดื่ม

As you can see, 3 of the above words have อ as the vowel placement consonant.

Example 1 - นึ่ง

In our first example we can clearly see Low Class initial consonant น, final consonant ง, and short vowel สระ ˉ:

$$/n/ + /ʉ/ + /ng/ = /nʉng/$$

Tone Mark

Low Class + Mái èek = *falling tone*

นึ่ง = nûng (*to be steamed* (food, cooking))

Sample Sentence

ฉันชอบทานผักนึ่ง

- ทาน – *to eat (*ทาน *is more polite than* กิน)
- ผัก – *vegetables*

I like eating steamed vegetables.

Example 2 – ดึง

This example switches to a Middle Class initial consonant with no tone mark:

/d/ + /ʉ/ + /ng/ = /dʉng/

- **HDL**
- **HLR**
- **MDL**
- **MLM**
- **LDSH**
- **LDLF**
- **LLM**

Tone Rules

Middle Class + Live syllable = *mid tone* (**MLM**)

ดึง= dʉng *(to pull, to draw, to haul)*

Sample Sentence

ห้ามดึงนะ

- ห้าม – *to forbid, to disallow, to prohibit, do not*

Don't pull it.

Example 3 – คือ

In this example we have the long vowel /ɯɯ/, our Low Class initial consonant ค, and the vowel placement consonant อ *(aw*ful (weather)):

$$/k/ + /ɯɯ/ + /silent/ = /kɯɯ/$$

Tone Mark

Low Class + Live syllable = *mid tone* (**LLM**)

คือ = kɯɯ *(to be)*

Sample Sentence

นั่นคือปากกาของฉัน

- ปากกา – *pen*

    That is my pen.

Example 4 – ผึ้ง

The initial consonant, though still making the same /p/ sound, is now a High Class consonant. The tone mark is Mái too:

$$/p/ + /ɯ/ + /ng/ = /pɯng/$$

Tone Mark

High Class + Mái too = *falling tone*

ผึ้ง = pɯ̂ng (*bee*)

ผมโดนผึ้งต่อยเมื่อวานนี้

- โดน – this indicates passive voice

- ต่อย – _to hit, to strike_

- เมื่อวานนี้ – _yesterday_

I was stung by a bee yesterday.

Example 5 – ซื้อ

The initial consonant has changed to Low Class ซ (/**s**/ as in **s**axophone

twins), then we have long vowel สระ ั้-, and then Middle Class อ in the ter-

minal position:

/**s**/ + /~~ʉʉ~~/ + /**silent**/ = /**s**~~ʉʉ~~/

Tone Mark

Low Class + Mái too = _high tone_

ซื้อ = s~~ʉʉ~~ (_to buy, to purchase_)

ฉันอยากซื้อบ้านสักหลัง

- สัก – an expression that refers to one

- หลัง – the classifier for house

I would like to buy a house.

Example 6 – หรือ

Now we can see that we have High Class consonant ห as an initial consonant, then ร, followed by อ, which we now know is silent when in the final position with this particular vowel. Is there an unwritten vowel between the ห and ร?

Remember, High Class ห followed by a Low Class consonant is more than likely going to mean there is a silent consonant here; and, it's a guarantee if the Low Class consonant is one of the *single sound consonants* (refer to Appendix E - Preceding Consonants on page 335):

- HDL
- HLR
- MDL
- MLM
- LDSH
- LDLF
- LLM

$$\textbf{/silent/ + /r/ + /}\textbf{uu}\textbf{/ + /silent/ = /}\underline{\textbf{ruu}}\textbf{/}$$

Tone Rules

High Class + Live syllable = *rising tone* (**HLR**)

หรือ = rǔu *(or)*

Sample Sentence

คุณต้องการกึ่งสุกหรือสุก

- กึ่งสุก – *rare*

- สุก – *well done*

Do you want rare or well-done?

Example 7 - ดื่ม

Now we see Middle Class consonant ด in the initial consonant position,

สระ $\overline{}$, Mái èek, and ม as the final consonant.

$$\text{/d/} + \text{/u̶u̶/} + \text{/m/} = \text{/d u̶u̶ m/}$$

Tone Mark

Middle Class + Mái èek = *low tone*

ดื่ม = dùum (*to drink*)

Sample Sentence

ผมดื่มน้ำเยอะมากแต่ละวัน

- เยอะ – *much, much more, a lot*

- แต่ละ – *each*

    I drink a lot of water each day.

Two Syllables/Words

- รู้สึก

- นับถือ

- หนังสือ

Example 8 – รู้สึก

We can see two written vowels in this example and can identify the syllables

quite clearly: สระ $_{\underset{\smile}{}}$ is always written underneath an initial consonant (in this case Low Class ร) and สระ ◌ื is always written above an initial consonant, in this case High Class ส. We see ก in the terminal consonant position (/**k**/).

$$\text{/r/} + \text{/uu/} + \text{/s/} + \text{/ʉ/} + \text{/k/} = \text{/ruu/-/sʉk/}$$

- HDL
- HLR
- MDL
- MLM
- LDSH
- LDLF
- LLM

Tone Rules

- Syllable 1: Low Class + Mái too = *high tone*
- Syllable 2: **H**igh Class + **D**ead syllable = *low tone* (**HDL**)

รู้สึก = rúu-sʉk (*to feel, to emote, to feel an emotion, to experience*)

<u>Sample Sentence</u>

ฉันรู้สึกเจ็บในอก

- เจ็บ – *pain, injured*
- อก – *chest, breast*

I feel pain in my chest.

Example 9 – นับถือ

There should be no difficulties here either. We have Low Class consonant น, Mái Hăn-aa-ġaat, Middle Class consonant บ, High Class consonant ถ (/**t**/ as in *tai*ls), then our long vowel, and our silent final consonant:

$$\text{/n/} + \text{/a/} + \text{/p/} + \text{/t/} + \text{/ʉʉ/} + \text{/silent/} = \text{/nap/-/tʉʉ/}$$

Tone Rules

- Syllable 1: **L**ow Class + **D**ead syllable and **SH**ort vowel = *high tone* (**LDSH**)

- Syllable 2: **High** Class + **L**ive syllable = *rising tone* (**HLR**)

นับถือ = náp-t<del>ŭŭ</del> *(to respect, to esteem, to revere, to reckon)*

<u>Sample Sentence</u>

ผมนับถืองานของเขา

- งาน = *work, job, task*

I respect his work.

Example 10 – หนังสือ

- HDL
- HLR
- MDL
- MLM
- LDSH
- LDLF
- LLM

A slight change to the previous example, where once again we see our silent

High Class consonant (ห) at the beginning of the word (and preceding a *single sound consonant*). The rest should be easy for you:

/**silent**/ + /n/ + /a/ + /ng/ + /s/ + /<del>ŭŭ</del>/ + /**silent**/ = /<u>n</u>ang/-/**sŭŭ**/

Tone Rules

- Syllable 1: **High** Class + **L**ive syllable = *rising tone* (**HLR**)
- Syllable 2: **High** Class + **L**ive syllable = *rising tone* (**HLR**)

หนังสือ = năng-s<del>ŭŭ</del> *(book, document, letters, alphabet, printed document, written document)*

<u>Sample Sentence</u>

หนังสือเล่มนี้เกี่ยวกับอะไร

- เล่ม – classifier for books, knives, candles
- เกี่ยวกับ – *about, regarding, concerning.*

What is this book about?

Exercise 12

Exercise 12a

Answers begin on page 346

Match the words to their meaning:

1.	ห้าม	pen	a.
2.	นิ่ง	work, job, task	b.
3.	ดื่ม	to pull, to draw, to haul	c.
4.	คือ	classifier for books, knives, candles	d.
5.	กึ่งสุก	classifier for a house	e.
6.	ผึ้ง	to drink	f.
7.	หนังสือ	to be	g.
8.	หลัง	or	h.
9.	ปากกา	(cooking) to be steamed	i.
10.	งาน	book, document, letters, etc.	j.
11.	เล่ม	pain, injured	k.
12.	หรือ	to disallow, to forbid, to prohibit	l.
13.	เจ็บ	rare	m.
14.	ดึง	to buy, to purchase	n
15.	ซื้อ	bee	o

Exercise 12b

Identify the syllables in these words (draw a vertical line, underline, or highlight the syllables):

1. ชื่อเล่น   4. ซื้อขาย   7. พื้นที่

2. ข้าศึก   5. ฝึกหัด   8. มือถือ

3. พึ่งพา   6. หรือเปล่า   9. สื่อสาร

1. ชื่อเล่น – *nickname*

2. ข้าศึก – *enemy*

3. พึ่งพา – *to rely on, to depend on*

4. ซื้อขาย – *to trade, to buy and sell, merchandise*

5. ฝึกหัด – *to drill, to practice, to train*

6. หรือเปล่า – *or not*

7. พื้นที่ – *district, area, place*

8. มือถือ – *cellphone, mobile phone*

9. สื่อสาร – *to communicate, to chat, to speak.*

Notes

สระ โ-ะ and สระ โ-

สระ โ-ะ and สระ โ- make the short /o/ as in *cot*, and the long /oo/ as in *ghost* sounds. We've encountered สระ โ-ะ many times so far, it's the unwritten vowel between two same syllable consonants.

How are they used?

The symbol โ is always written before an initial consonant and like many of the vowels, with a little practice you will start to see it instantly.

One Syllable Words

- โต๊ะ
- โต
- โกรธ
- โลก

- โชค
- โดย
- โรง
- โปรด

Example 1 – โต๊ะ

Mái Dtrii (ʹ)

makes the syllable or word high tone.

We are only using one example of the short vowel in this section, with Middle Class ต (remember this sound is /**dt**/, not /**d**/), and a tone mark that we haven't seen before in these chapters. I hope you can remember it? This tone mark is called *Mái dtrii* and it makes the tone of the syllable it is in *high tone*.

$$/\text{dt}/ + /\text{o}/ = /\text{dto}/$$

Tone Mark

Any consonant class + Mái dtrii = *high tone*

โต๊ะ = dtó *(table)*

Sample Sentence

กระเป๋าของคุณอยู่บนโต๊ะของฉัน

- กระเป๋า – *bag, pocket*

        Your bag is on my table.

Example 2 – โต

In this example, we use the same consonant and the long vowel /**oo**/:

$$/\text{dt}/ + /\text{oo}/ = /\text{dtoo}/$$

- HDL
- HLR
- MDL
- MLM
- LDSH
- LDLF
- LLM

Tone Rules

Middle Class + Live syllable = *mid tone* (**MLM**)

โต = dtoo *(big, large, grown)*

Sample Sentence

ฉันอยากเป็นครูเมื่อฉันโตขึ้น

- เมื่อ – *when*

    I would like to be a teacher when I grow up.

Example 3 – โกรธ

Consonant Clusters
begin with

ก, ข, ค, ต,

ป, ผ, *or* พ.

*The second consonant is **always***
ร, ล, *or* ว.

Whenever you see Middle Class consonant ก followed by another consonant, hopefully you're getting into the habit of looking to see if it forms a consonant cluster. Remember, if the second consonant is ร, ล, or ว then it will most likely be a cluster (one exception we've already seen is in the chapter on Unwritten Vowels and example 2, กรุณา, there is no consonant cluster here). The terminal consonant in this example is Low Class:

/gr/ + /oo/ + /t/ = /groot/

Tone Rules

Middle Class + **D**ead syllable = *low tone* (**MDL**)

โกรธ = gròot *(mad, angry)*

Sample Sentence

คุณโกรธผมเหรอ

- เหรอ – question particle when seeking confirmation or truth

    Are you mad at me?

Example 4 – โลก

This is a very simple word made up of two consonants we have seen many times before:

$$/l/ + /oo/ + /k/ = /look/$$

- HDL
- HLR
- MDL
- MLM
- LDSH
- LDLF
- LLM

Tone Rules

Low Class + Dead syllable and Long vowel = *falling tone* (**LDLF**)

โลก = lôok (the planet *Earth*, *the world*)

Sample Sentence

โลกกำลังร้อนขึ้น

- ร้อน – *hot, warm*

   The earth is getting warmer.

Example 5 – โชค

In this example, we have two more familiar Low Class consonants:

$$/ch/ + /oo/ + /k/ = /chook/$$

Tone Rules

Low Class + Dead syllable and Long vowel = *falling tone* (**LDLF**)

โชค = chôok *(luck)*

Sample Sentence

โชคดีนะ

Good luck.

Example 6 – โดย

Again, no surprises here. We have a familiar Middle Class consonant in the initial consonant position and a familiar Low Class consonant in the terminal position:

$$/d/ + /oo/ + /i/ = /dooi/$$

Tone Rules

Middle Class + Live syllable = *m*id tone (**MLM**)

โดย = dooi *(by, via, route, way)*

<u>Sample Sentence</u>

พวกเราไปภูเก็ตโดยเครื่องบิน

- เครื่องบิน – *aeroplane*

    We went to Phuket by plane.

Example 7 – โรง

Here we have another two common Low Class consonants:

$$/r/ + /oo/ + /ng/ = /roong/$$

Tone Rules

Low Class + Live syllable = *m*id tone (**LLM**)

- โรง = roong *(building, hall, pavilion, structure)*

 Sample Sentence

แม่ของฉันกำลังไปที่โรงนา

- โรงนา – *farm shed, farm shack*

  My mother is going to the farm shed.

Example 8 – โปรด

Consonant Clusters
begin with

ก, ข, ค, ต,

ป, ผ, *or* พ.

The second consonant is **always**
ร, ล, *or* ว.

We see we only have a single vowel in this word and 3 consonants. As mentioned before, whenever you see ร as a second consonant, always suspect a possible consonant cluster (Table 4, page 17).

$$/bpr/ + /oo/ + /t/ = /bproot/$$

Tone Rules

Middle Class + **D**ead syllable = *low tone* (**MDL**)

โปรด = bpròot (*please*)

Sample Sentence

โปรดระวัง

- ระวัง – *to watch out for, careful, cautious*

  Please be careful.

Two Syllable Words

- โรงเรียน

- ยุโรป

Example 9 – โรงเรียน

Here we can see the word we used in example 7 as the first syllable/word; this leaves us with เรียน. We don't cover this vowel until page 257, but if you remember the sound it makes (from *MATYGA*, the application, or from the list of consonants in Table 3 on page 16), it makes the /**iia**/ as in *reind**eer*** sound:

$$/\textbf{roong}/ + /\textbf{r}/ + /\textbf{iia}/ + /\textbf{n}/ = /\textbf{roong}/\text{-}/\textbf{riian}/$$

- HDL
- HLR
- MDL
- MLM
- LDSH
- LDLF
- LLM

Tone Rules

Without any tone marks, we calculate tone. Both syllables are:

Low Class + Live syllable = *mid tone* (**LLM**)

โรงเรียน = roong- riian *(school)*

Sample Sentence

ฉันรักโรงเรียนของฉัน

I love my school.

Example 10 – ยุโรป

This word is a little different to those we have used before as examples. We can clearly see two vowels, the first of which we've already covered. As สระ

◌ุ is always written beneath an initial consonant, and สระ โ- always marks the beginning of a syllable of word, identifying the two syllable/words is simple.

The first consonant of the second syllable (ร) is <u>never</u> an initial consonant in a consonant cluster (Table 3), so we now know that ป has to be a terminal consonant:

/y/ + /u/ + /r/ + /oo/ + /p/ = /yu/-/roop/

- HDL
- HLR
- MDL
- MLM
- LDSH
- LDLF
- LLM

Tone Rules

- Syllable 1: **L**ow Class + **D**ead syllable and **S**hort vowel = *high tone* (**LDSH**)

- Syllable 2: **L**ow Class + **D**ead syllable and **L**ong vowel = *falling tone* (**LDLF**)

ยุโรป = yú- rôop (this is the Thai transcription of *"Europe"*)

<u>*Sample Sentence*</u>

ผมอยากไปเที่ยวยุโรป

- เที่ยว – *to go out, to travel, to tour*

I would like to travel to Europe.

Exercise 13

Exercise 13a

Answers begin on page 346

Match the words to their meaning:

1.	กระเป๋า	school	a.
2.	เครื่องบิน	table	b.
3.	โกรธ	bag, pocket	c.
4.	โรงเรียน	by, via, route, way	d.
5.	โรงนา	big, large, grown	e.
6.	เมื่อ	hot, warm	f.
7.	โดย	want	g.
8.	โต๊ะ	planet Earth, the world	h.
9.	โรง	aeroplane	i.
10.	โชค	luck	j.
11.	โต	farm shed, shack	k.
12.	ร้อน	when	l.
13.	โลก	angry, mad	m.
14.	อยาก	to go out, to travel, to tour	n
15.	เที่ยว	building, hall, pavilion, structure	o

Exercise 13b

Identify the syllables in these words (draw a vertical line, underline, or high-light the syllables):

1. ชั่วโมง	4. โรงเรียน	7. โกรธง่าย
2. โบราณ	5. สิงโต	8. โมทนา
3. ประโยชน์	6. โอกาส	9. ความโกลาหล

The word meanings are:

1. ชั่วโมง – *hour*

2. โบราณ – *ancient*

3. ประโยชน์ – *benefit, usefulness*

4. โรงเรียน – *school*

5. สิงโต – *lion*

6. โอกาส – *chance, opportunity, occasion*

7. โกรธง่าย – *to be sensitive, easily annoyed*

8. โมทนา – *pleased, rejoice, delighted*

9. ความโกลาหล – *mayhem, pandemonium, riotousness.*

Notes

สระ เ-ะ and สระ แ-ะ

These two vowels are short vowels and as we have already looked at their long vowel equivalents, สระ เ- and สระ แ-, have been grouped together into this single section.

สระ เ-ะ makes the short /e/ as in *net* sound, and สระ แ-ะ makes the short /ɛ/ as in *trap* sound.

How are they used?

We talked earlier about how short vowel สระ -ะ can be used to shorten certain vowels and we have seen in many of the previous posts how this is applied.

We know สระ -ะ marks the end of a syllable or a word, and we know สระ เ- and สระ แ- are always written before an initial consonant. All we have to do is look and see if these vowels belong to the same syllable/word; if they do, then the vowel will be the short vowel equivalent สระ เ-ะ or สระ แ-ะ.

One Syllable Words

- เละ
- และ
- แนะ

- แกะ
- แยะ

Example 1 - เละ

Here we see Low Class ล and short vowel สระ เ-ะ (/e/), this gives us:

$$/l/ + /e/ = /le/$$

- HDL
- HLR
- MDL
- MLM
- LDSH
- LDLF
- LLM

Tone Rules

Low Class + Dead syllable and Short vowel = *high tone* (**LDSH**)

เละ = lé *(soft, mushy)*

Sample Sentence

ข้าวจานนี้เละไปหน่อย

This plate of rice is a bit mushy.

Example 2 - และ

In this example we change the vowel to สระ แ-ะ (/ɛ/):

$$/l/ + /ɛ/ = /lɛ/$$

Tone Rules

Low Class + Dead syllable and Short vowel = *high tone* (**LDSH**)

และ = lɛ́ *(and)*

Sample Sentence

ช่วยส่งน้ำตาลและน้ำปลาให้หน่อยค่ะ

- ส่ง - *to send, to pass something to someone*

  Can you pass me sugar and fish sauce please?

Example 3 - แนะ

Here we switch the consonant to น:

$$/n/ + /\varepsilon/ = /n\varepsilon/$$

Tone Rules

Once more we see a familiar pattern:

Low Class + **D**ead syllable and **S**hort vowel = *high tone* (**LDSH**)

แนะ = né *(to advise, to suggest, to guide)*

Sample Sentence

เขาแนะแต่สิ่งดีๆ ให้เพื่อนของเขา

(It's a short version of แนะนำ)

- แต่ – *only, just, but*
- สิ่งดีๆ – *good thing*

He only suggests good things for his friends.

Example 4 - แกะ

Switching across to the first consonant in the Thai alphabet, we have:

$$/g/ + /\varepsilon/ = /g\varepsilon/$$

Tone Rules

Middle Class + **D**ead syllable = *low tone* (**MDL**)

แกะ = gè *(to unwrap, to unbind, to engrave, to carve, sheep, ewe, ram)*

Sample Sentence

ฉันขอแกะของขวัญวันเกิดตอนนี้ได้ไหม

- ของขวัญ – _gift, present_

- วันเกิด – _birthday_

May I unwrap my birthday present now?

Note: _it may feel like we're just building vocabulary here, but these exercises help to reinforce that the vowel sound <u>stays the same</u> regardless of the other consonants in the syllable or word; and, it always helps to look at the sentence structure and new vocabulary._

Two Syllables/Words

- เละเทะ

- แนะนำ

- แกะรอย

Example 5 - เละเทะ

From what we've covered so far, we can easily see this compound word is made up of two syllables/words:

- HDL
- HLR
- MDL
- MLM
- LDSH
- LDLF
- LLM

/l/ + /e/ - /t/ + /e/ = /le/-/te/

Tone Rules

- Syllable 1: **L**ow Class + **D**ead syllable and **S**hort vowel = _high tone_ (**LDSH**)

- Syllable 2: **L**ow Class + **D**ead syllable and **S**hort vowel = *high tone* (**LDSH**)

เละเทะ = lέ-tέ *(to disarrange, dirty, filthy, untidy)*

Sample Sentence

บ้านดูเละเทะมากเลย

The house looks so filthy.

Example 6 - แนะนำ

It should be getting repetitively easy with these vowels now. In this example, we can quite easily see the two syllable/words:

$$/n/ + /ɛ/ - /n/ + /am/ = /nɛ/-/nam/$$

Tone Rules

- Syllable 1: **L**ow Class + **D**ead syllable and **S**hort vowel = *high tone* (**LDSH**)

- Syllable 2: **L**ow Class + **L**ive syllable = *mid tone* (**LLM**)

แนะนำ = nέ-nam *(to introduce someone, to advise, to suggest, to guide)*

Sample Sentence

เขาแนะนำฉันให้รู้จักกับจอห์น

She introduced me to John.

Example 7- แกะรอย

In the last example of this section, we have already encountered the first syllable/word (example 4); and, in the second syllable word, we see the Middle

สระ -อ

Often when you encounter อ in the middle of 2 other consonants, it will be acting as a vowel.

Class consonant อ. We know it can also function as a vowel; but, unless we know the word itself we have to work out what role it is performing.

If อ was acting as a consonant then there would need to be an unwritten /a/ before it (rule 8), and an unwritten /o/ after it (rule 7); but, this is rare. However, unless you knew the sound that this word made either you have to ask someone, look it up in a dictionary, or hazard a guess. Here, อ is acting as a vowel:

$$/g/ + /\varepsilon/ - /r/ + /ɔɔ/ + /i/ = /g\varepsilon/-/rɔɔi/$$

Tone Rules

- HDL
- HLR
- MDL
- MLM
- LDSH
- LDLF
- LLM

- Syllable 1: **M**iddle Class + **D**ead syllable = *low tone* (**MDL**)
- Syllable 2: **L**ow Class + **L**ive syllable = *mid tone* (**LLM**)

แกะรอย = gɛ̀-rɔɔi (*to trace, to detect*)

Sample Sentence

ตำรวจกำลังพยายามแกะรอยเด็กผู้หญิงที่หายตัวไป

- ตำรวจ – *police*

- พยายาม – to *try, to attempt*

- เด็กผู้หญิง – *girl*

- หายตัว – *to disappear, to vanish, invisible*

    Police are trying to trace the missing girl.

Exercise 14

Exercise 14a

Answers begin on page 347

Match the words to their meaning:

1.	เละ	birthday	a.
2.	แนะ	girl	b.
3.	วันเกิด	fish sauce	c.
4.	จาน	soft, mushy	d.
5.	เละเทะ	to advise, to suggest	e.
6.	เด็กผู้หญิง	and	f.
7.	ตำรวจ	now	g.
8.	ตอนนี้	to introduce someone, to advise, to suggest, to guide	h.
9.	และ	police	i.
10.	บ้าน	only, just, but	j.
11.	เขา	plate	k.
12.	น้ำปลา	house	l.
13.	ส่ง	filthy, dirty, untidy	m.
14.	แต่	he, she, him, her	n
15.	แนะนำ	to send, to pass something to someone	o

It is very easy to discern syllables in words containing these vowels, so there's very little point in providing this kind of exercise here. What we will do is ask you to identify the unwritten vowel.

Exercise 14b

Identify the unwritten vowel in these compound words (there is only 1 unwritten vowel in each word) and work out the tone of each syllable/word:

1. สงสัย - /s/ + /o/ + /ng/ - /s/ + /a/ + /i/ = /song-sai/

- Syllable 1: **High Class** + **Live** syllable = *rising tone* (**HLR**)
- Syllable 2: **High Class** + **Live** syllable = *rising tone* (**HLR**)

2. ฉบับ

3. จดหมาย

4. มนุษย์

5. ชนิด

6. ประชาชน

Notes

สระ เ-าะ and สระ -อ

These are the last 2 of the 20 simple vowels in the Thai alphabet. After these, there are only 12 complex vowels left to do. We sincerely hope at this point that you can see how easy it is to break down sentences once you can identify the vowels.

With the short vowel, be aware that สระ เ-าะ is <u>not</u> the short vowel version of สระ เ-า. We know full well that one of the roles of สระ −ะ is to shorten vowels, and though that's exactly what it is doing here, สระ เ-า itself <u>does not have a short vowel equivalent</u>.

As we know, the long vowel สระ -อ can cause confusion as it has a number of other roles. We've encountered this a few times so far and I hope that with these examples you can see that by knowing and adhering to the rules, it isn't overly difficult to discern the actual function each time. สระ เ-าะ makes the short /ɔ/ as in s*lot* sound, and สระ -อ makes the long /ɔɔ/ as in **aw***ful* [weather] sound.

How are they used?

We have seen many examples where the component parts of สระ เ-าะ (เ-า and -ะ) are used, and สระ เ-าะ follows the exact same rules as สระ เ-า (page 147). สระ -อ is always written after a consonant, which means that if you encounter a word such as ออก, the first อ <u>cannot</u> be a vowel (it must be a vowel placement consonant).

One Syllable Words

- เกาะ
- เพราะ
- ห้อง
- ออก

- ร้อย
- หน่อย
- ของ

Example 1 - เกาะ

Here we see the short vowel สระ เ-าะ (/ɔ/) and Middle Class ก. This gives us:

$$/g/ + /ɔ/ = /gɔ/$$

- HDL
- HLR
- MDL
- MLM
- LDSH
- LDLF
- LLM

Tone Rules

Middle Class + **D**ead syllable = *low tone* (**MDL**)

เกาะ = gɔ̀ *(island, to hold, to lay hold of, to rest on)*

Sample Sentence

เกาะช้างสวยมาก

Koh Chang island is very beautiful.

Example 2 – เพราะ

As we can see that our short สระ เ-าะ vowel has 2 consonants between it, we straightaway know that พร is a consonant cluster. If necessary, we can always confirm this by looking at Table 4.

$$/pr/ + /ɔ/ = /prɔ/$$

Tone Rules

Low Class + Dead syllable and Short vowel = *high tone* (**LDSH**)

เพราะ = prɔ́ *(because, because of, due to, owing to)*

Sample Sentence

ฉันไม่ได้ไปงานเลี้ยงเพราะฉันรู้สึกไม่สบาย

- งานเลี้ยง – *party, festival, feast, banquet*

  I didn't go to the party because I was feeling unwell.

Example 3 – ห้อง

Now we have a High Class initial consonant (/**h**/ as in *humps*) with Mái too, the vowel สระ -อ, and Low Class ง as the terminal consonant.

/h/ + /ɔɔ/ + /ng/ = /hɔɔng/

Tone Mark

High Class + Mái too = *falling tone*

ห้อง = hɔ̂ɔng *(room of a building, apartment, chamber)*

Sample Sentence

ผมชอบการตกแต่งของห้องนั่งเล่นนี้

- การตกแต่ง - *decoration*

  I like the decoration of this sitting room.

Example 4 – ออก

As we mentioned in the 'How are they Used' section, the vowel สระ -อ is always written after a consonant; therefore, the first letter in this word has to be a vowel placement consonant.

/silent/ + /ɔɔ/ + /k/ = /ɔ̲ɔ̲k̲/

Tone Rules

Middle Class + **D**ead syllable = *low tone* (**MDL**)

ออก = ɔ̀ɔk *(it means to go out, to get out, to exit)*

<u>*Sample Sentence*</u>

ออกทางไหนครับ

Which way to get out?

Example 5 – ร้อย

This example is very straightforward with a Low Class initial consonant, Mái too, our featured long vowel, and a Low Class terminal consonant.

/r/ + /ɔɔ/ + /i/ = /rɔɔi/

- HDL
- HLR
- MDL
- MLM
- LDSH
- LDLF
- LLM

Tone Rules

Low Class + Mái too = *high tone*

ร้อย = rɔ́ɔi *(hundred, the number one hundred, 100)*

Sample Sentence

คุณมีเงิน 100 บาทไหม

Do you have 100 baht?

Example 6 - หน่อย

We have seen this word in previous examples but we'll examine the actual word structure a bit more here.

Compared to the last example we have a change of tone mark and a different initial consonant. Remember, one of the functions of High Class ห is as a preceding consonant; and, if ห was a spoken consonant, then it would require an unwritten vowel between it and น; however, it isn't, and we don't.

The tone mark (in this case Mái èek) is always written over the initial consonant of a syllable; and, as ห is silent, these form a kind of consonant cluster at the start of the word (they are not strictly a cluster, but it helps to frame the idea), and are treated as one consonant. This gives us:

/silent/ + /n/ + /ɔɔ/ + /i/ = /nɔɔi/

Tone Mark

High Class + Mái èek = *low tone*

หน่อย = nɔ̀ɔi ([this is a word which is used to
soften the meaning of a sentence]
"...a bit", "...somewhat", "...to some extent")

Sample Sentence

ฉันขอยืมปากกาหน่อยได้ไหมค่ะ

May I borrow your pen?

Example 7 - ของ

After the last few examples, this one is very straightforward with a High Class initial consonant and a Low Class final consonant. If you're unsure of whether the อ is a vowel or a consonant, refer back to example 4 in this section.

$$/k/ + /ɔɔ/ + /ng/ = /kɔɔng/$$

- HDL
- HLR
- MDL
- MLM
- LDSH
- LDLF
- LLM

Tone Rules

High Class + **Live** syllable = *rising tone* (**HLR**)

ของ = kǒɔng (*of, belonging to, that or those of*)

Sample Sentence

รถของเขาสีขาว

Her car is white.

or

รถของดวงตาสีขาว

Duangta's car is white.

Two Syllables/Words

- ตลอด

- ข้างนอก

- รองเท้า

Example 8 – ตลอด

We know from our previous examples, that when we see อ between 2 consonants, unless we can also see written vowels there is a good chance that อ is acting as a vowel.

Rule 8
*Unwritten /a/ occurs between 2 consonants in **different syllables**.*

Knowing this helps us identify the 2nd syllable in this example; and, now we can clearly see there is only one unwritten vowel between the first and second consonants (ต and ล). As they are clearly in different syllables, the unwritten vowel has to be /a/.

$$/dt/ + /a/ + /silent/ + /l/ + /ɔɔ/ + /t/ = /dta\text{-}l\underline{ɔɔ}t/$$

Tone Rules

- Syllable 1: **M**iddle Class + **D**ead syllable = *low tone* (**MDL**)
- Syllable 2: **H**igh Class + **D**ead syllable = *low tone* (**HDL**)

* I know the second syllable begins with Low Class ล but, if you remember before, we quoted the *Preceding Consonants* rule. This rule also states that if a word begins with a Middle Class consonant and is followed by a syllable that begins with a Low Class single consonant, then unwritten ห is used before that Low Class syllable (refer to Appendix E - Preceding Consonants for further details).

Preceding Consonants
It's really helpful for you to understand these rules, so if you haven't read this section, please do so.

ตลอด = dtà-lɔ̀ɔt *(throughout, through, in, e.g., in over 20 years)*

Sample Sentence

เขาพูดตลอดการเดินทาง

She talked all throughout the journey.

Example 9 – ข้างนอก

In this example, we can see two long vowels: สระ -า and สระ -อ. Both of these have an initial and a final consonant and we can easily identify our two syllables/words.

$$/k/ + /aa/ + /ng/ - /n/ + /ɔɔ/ + /k/ = /kaang/-/nɔɔk/$$

- HDL
- HLR
- MDL
- MLM
- LDSH
- LDLF
- LLM

Tone Rules

- Syllable 1: **High Class** + **M**ái too = *falling tone*

- Syllable 2: **Low Class** + **Dead syllable and Long vowel** = *falling tone* (**LDLF**)

$$ข้างนอก = kâang-nɔ̂ɔk (outside, external)$$

Sample Sentence

$$กรุณารอข้างนอก$$

- รอ - *to wait (for)*

Please wait outside.

Example 10 – รองเท้า

The final example in this section shouldn't cause any problems and we'll go straight into the sounds:

$$/r/ + /ɔɔ/ + /ng/ + /t/ + /ao/ = /rɔɔng/-/tao/$$

Tone Rules

- Syllable 1: **Low Class** + **Live syllable** = *mid tone* (**LLM**)

- Syllable 2: **Low Class** + **Dead syllable and Short vowel** = *high tone* (**LDSH**)

$$รองเท้า = rɔɔng-táo (shoes, footwear)$$

Sample Sentence

กรุณาถอดรองเท้า

- ถอด - *to take off, to remove, to interpret, to translate*

Please take off your shoes.

Exercise 15

Exercise 15a

Answers begin on page 348

Match the words to their meaning:

1.	ร้อย	very beautiful	a.
2.	ถอด	belonging to, of	b.
3.	เกาะ	room of a building, apartment, chamber	c.
4.	หน่อย	island	d.
5.	ของ	pen	e.
6.	สวยมาก	to exit, to get out, to go out	f.
7.	ตลอด	to wait for	g.
8.	รองเท้า	Thai currency	h.
9.	รอ	word made to make a sentence softer/more polite	i.
10.	เพราะ	throughout, through, in	j.
11.	ปากกา	to take off, to remove	k.
12.	ข้างนอก	100	l.
13.	ห้อง	shoes	m.
14.	บาท	outside, external	n
15.	ออก	because	o

Exercise 15b

Identify the syllables in these words. Most of the words here are fairly uncommon but the exercise is to identify the syllables using the rules you now know. Number 6 has 4 syllables, and we've already covered 3 of the vowels in this word:

1. เกาะสมุย   3. เพาะชำ   5. เจาะจงชื่อ

2. เกาะกลาง   4. เพราะฉะนั้น   6. เพาะเลี้ยงสัตว์น้ำ

The word meanings are:

1. เกาะสมุย – *Gɔ̀ Sàmui* (Samui island - a popular holiday destination)

2. เกาะกลาง – *street island, traffic island*

3. เพาะชำ – *to plant, to sow, to cultivate*

4. เพราะฉะนั้น – *so, consequently, therefore*

5. เจาะจงชื่อ – *to specify by name, to mention.*

6. เพาะเลี้ยงสัตว์น้ำ – *to raise aquatic animals*

Complex Vowels

สระ เ-อะ and สระ เ-อ

These are the first 2 of the 12 complex vowels. The short vowel in this and the next 3 sections are <u>very uncommon</u> – you will rarely see them.

สระ เ-อะ makes the /ə/ as in *above* sound and สระ เ-อ makes the /əə/ as in ***ear**ly* sound.

How are they used?

As can be seen from the component parts of these vowels, we have one familiar vowel that is always written before the consonant (สระ เ-), and we have สระ -อ written after the consonant.

Although สระ เ- is a vowel on its own, it is also the first part in a number of complex vowels; and, as such, when you see สระ เ-, you need to get into the habit of looking to see what other vowels are written above or after the initial consonant/cluster as these could determine the actual vowel being used.

As mentioned before, if you encounter short สระ -ะ, it performs one of its usual functions of shortening a long vowel.

Note: no other vowels are ever used with vowels written beneath consonants (สระ ◌ุ or สระ ◌ู), these always operate solo.

One Syllable Words

- เลอะ

- เยอะ

- เสมอ

- เรอ

Example 1 – เลอะ

This example shows Low Class ล and the short vowel (/ə/):

$$/l/ + /ə/ = /lə/$$

Tone Rules

Low Class + **D**ead syllable and **S**hort vowel = **h**igh tone (**LDSH**)

เลอะ = lə́ *(stained, soiled, untidy)*

<u>Sample Sentence</u>

ห้ามทำเสื้อเลอะนะ

Don't stain your shirt.

Example 2 - เยอะ

Swapping the consonant to Low Class ย we have:

$$/y/ + /ə/ = /yə/$$

Tone Rules

Low Class + **D**ead syllable and **S**hort vowel = **h**igh tone (**LDSH**)

เยอะ = yə́ *(many, much, abundant)*

<u>*Sample Sentence*</u>

คุณเอาข้าวเยอะไหม

Do you want much rice?

Example 3 - เสมอ

Example 3 doesn't comply with any of the rules we've covered before in this book.

If you look at this word, the vowel and the consonants, you may have first tried to work out whether there is a consonant cluster here; but, glancing at Table 4 shows us that High Class ส and Low Class ม never form consonant clusters.

Next, you may have made a guess that สระ เ- and สระ -อ are separate vowels; but, the vowel here is สระ เ-อ.

Last, after you've finished puzzling over these, you may come up with something else we didn't; but, once again, it's down to the *preceding consonants* rules (page 335).

Before we explain what's occurring here, we must point out that this is the most complex process which we've yet encountered in the Thai language. We have never seen this written on any English website or in any English book that teaches Thai. It's a construct from our translation of the Thai process and trying to make sense of the flow. It may not be 100% in all instances, but we hope you can follow the general idea. Step-by-step, the process is as follows:

1. Is there more than one consonant?

   a. If yes, go to 2.

b. If no, then there is a single vowel - end here.

2. Is there a consonant cluster?

   a. If yes, then there is a single vowel - end here.

   b. If no, goto 3.

3. Is the initial consonant either High Class ห, or Middle Class อ?

   a. If yes, goto 4.

   b. If the answer is no, goto 5.

4. Is the initial consonant followed by a single sound consonant?

   a. If yes, then ห, or อ is acting as a silent consonant to modify the syllable/word tone of the single sound consonant.

   b. If no, goto 5.

5. The two consonants do not form a cluster, but the preceding consonant rule applies and unwritten ห is used before the Low Class consonant. In addition, the initial High Class consonant is followed by unwritten vowel /a/ between it and the second syllable. This is exactly what is happening in our example:

Solution

Let's look at this and our example (เสมอ) in detail:

Again, this is an extremely complicated process to explain; our advice is to be aware it exists, but don't get hung-up on it.

1. Is there more than one consonant?

If the syllable or word is comprised of a single consonant, then the vowel has to be a single vowel; however, if there are 2 consonants then we need to know if they form a consonant cluster. Our example has more than 1 consonant, so go to step 2.

2. Is there a consonant cluster?

If they do form a consonant cluster, it means the vowel is สระ เ-อ. In our example, there is no consonant cluster (ส and ม do not form clusters), go to step 3.

3. Is the initial consonant either High Class ห, or Middle Class อ?

If there is a consonant cluster, then the cluster is treated as a single consonant and the vowel is our complex vowel (สระ เ-อ), i.e. it is not split into separate components.

With our example, we know the consonants don't form a cluster (from 2) so now we need to see if the initial consonant is there as a silent/preceding consonant. In our example, the initial consonant is not ห or อ so it is not there to act as a silent consonant (we can miss out step 4), goto 5.

5. The two consonants do not form a cluster, but the preceding consonant rule applies and unwritten ห is used before the Low Class consonant. In addition, the initial High Class consonant is followed by unwritten vowel /**a**/ between it and the second syllable. This is exactly what is happening in our example:

เสมอ = สะ-เหมอ

/**s**/ + /**a**/ + /**silent**/ + /**m**/ + /**əə**/ = /**sa**/-/**məə**/

Tone Rules

- HDL
- HLR
- MDL
- MLM
- LDSH
- LDLF
- LLM

- Syllable 1: **H**igh Class + **D**ead syllable = *low tone* (**HDL**)
- Syllable 2: **H**igh Class + **L**ive syllable = *rising tone* (**HLR**)

เสมอ = sà-mǒə (*always*)

เราทานอาหารเย็นด้วยกันเสมอ

We always have dinner together.

As we mentioned, this is quite easily the most complicated process we've encountered in Thai to date. The easiest way around it is just to learn and recognise the word. To be honest, don't get too hung up on it, just be aware that the rule exists.

Example 4 - เรอ

This example shouldn't pose too many problems, it's Low Class ร and the long vowel:

$$/r/ + /əə/ = /rəə/$$

Tone Rules

Low Class + Live syllable = *mid tone* (**LLM**)

เรอ = rəə *(to burp, to belch)*

<u>*Sample Sentence*</u>

เขาเรอดังมากหลังอาหารเย็น

He burped very loud after dinner.

Two Syllables/Words

* เกรอะกรัง

* กันเถอะ

* เพ้อเจ้อ

Example 5 - เกรอะกรัง

The short vowel is quite unique and is hard to mistake. Looking at the first syllable/word, we see Middle Class ก followed immediately by Low Class ร

Complex Vowels

and seeing this combination will hopefully trigger 'consonant cluster'. That's the first syllable/word done.

Consonant Clusters
begin with

ก, ข, ค, ต,

ป, ผ, *or* พ.

*The second consonant is **always***
ร, ล, *or* ว.

Again, we see the same two consonants so we know that this is likely to be another cluster. Our second clue is Mái Hăn-aa-ġaat (อั-) which, as we know, is a medial vowel so it needs both an initial and a final consonant:

/gr/ + /ə/ + /gr/ + /a/ + /ng/ = /grə/-/grang/

Tone Rules

- Syllable 1: **M**iddle Class + **D**ead syllable = *low tone* (**MDL**)
- Syllable 2: **M**iddle Class + **L**ive syllable = *mid tone* (**MLM**)

เกรอะกรัง = grə̀-grang (*matted into a lump*)

<u>Sample Sentence</u>

คราบสกปรกเกาะเกรอะกรังบนพื้นห้องน้ำ

- คราบสกปรก – *dirty stain*

    A dirty stain is matted into a lump on the bathroom floor.

Example 6 – กันเถอะ

With Mái Hăn-aa-ġaat fresh in your mind, this word shouldn't pose any problems:

/g/ + /a/ + /n/ + /t/ + /ə/ = /gan/-/tə/

Tone Rules

- Syllable 1: **M**iddle Class + **L**ive syllable = *mid tone* (**MLM**)
- Syllable 2: **H**igh Class + **D**ead syllable = *low tone* (**HDL**)

กันเถอะ = gan-tə̀ (*let's*)

Sample Sentence

คืนนี้ไปดูหนังกันเถอะ

Let's go to the cinema tonight.

Example 7 - เพ้อเจ้อ

Here we can see our long vowel and Mái too repeated in each syllable/word:

/p/ + /əə/ - /j/ + /əə/ = /pəə/-/jəə/

- HDL
- HLR
- MDL
- MLM
- LDSH
- LDLF
- LLM

Tone Rules

- Syllable 1: Low Class + Mái too = *high tone*

- Syllable 2: Middle Class + Mái too = *falling tone*

เพ้อเจ้อ = péə–jêə (*to talk nonsense*)

Sample Sentence

อย่าพูดเพ้อเจ้อ

Don't talk nonsense.

Exercise 16

Exercise 16a

Answers begin on page 348

Match the words to their meaning:

1.	มี	always	a.
2.	กันเถอะ	shirt, blouse, t-shirt	b.
3.	พูด	to have	c.
4.	อาหารเย็น	don't, do not	d.
5.	เสื้อ	much, many, abundant	e.
6.	ไปดูหนัง	to talk nonsense	f.
7.	อย่า	let's	g.
8.	เสมอ	to go see a movie	h.
9.	ดังมาก	stained, soiled, untidy	i.
10.	คืนนี้	to talk	j.
11.	ห้องน้ำ	very loud	k.
12.	เลอะ	dinner	l.
13.	เพ้อเจ้อ	bathroom	m.
14.	เรอ	tonight	n
15.	เยอะ	to burp, to belch	o

Exercise 16b

Identify the unwritten vowels in these words and calculate the tone for each syllable The first one should be easy for you, but you need to know the preceding consonants rules for the remainder (refer to page 335.).

1. ส้มตำ

2. ขนาด

3. ถวาย

4. ทหาร

5. บริการ

6. ถนน

Notes

สระ เ-ียะ and สระ เ-ีย

Bearing in mind what was mentioned about looking for vowels above and after the initial consonant when you encounter สระ เ-, these vowels illustrate this perfectly.

Short vowel, สระ เ-ียะ, is the second of the four vowels that are very rare in Thai; therefore, as long as you know the long vowel sound, are aware that a short vowel equivalent exists and know the shortening role which สระ -ะ performs, you should have little problem remembering this.

สระ เ-ียะ makes the /ia/ as in *ria* sound, and สระ เ-ีย makes the /iia/ as in *reindeer* sound.

How are they used?

As mentioned, though the short vowel is very rare, the long vowel is very common. With practice, it is another one that will eventually jump out of the page at you. สระ เ-ีย is comprised of three separate parts: สระ เ-, สระ -ี, and ย. Like all vowel sounds in Thai, regardless of the consonant that this vowel is written 'with', the consonant sound is pronounced first, and the vowel sound <u>stays the same.</u>

One Syllable Words

- เมีย

- เที่ยง

- เที่ยว

- เปลี่ยน

- เลี้ยง

- เสีย

Example 1 – เมีย

This word is very easy to read. We have a familiar Low Class consonant and our complex vowel:

$$/m/ + /iia/ = /miia/$$

Tone Rules

Low Class + Live syllable = *mid tone* (**LLM**)

เมีย = miia (*wife* - informal)

Sample Sentence

เขาซื้อแหวนเพชรให้เมียของเขา

He bought his wife a diamond ring.

Example 2 – เที่ยง

Here we have a different combination:

$$/t/ + /iia/ + /ng/ = /tiiang/$$

Tone Mark

Low Class + Mái èek = *falling tone*

เที่ยง = tîiang *(1200 hours, 12 p.m, noon)*

ผมมีนัดพบหมอตอนเที่ยง

- นัดพบ - *make an appointment with*

    I have an appointment with the doctor at noon.

Example 3 – เที่ยว

Swapping over the final consonant gives us:

/t/ + /iia/ + /o/ = /tiiao/

Tone Mark

Low Class + Mái èek = *falling tone*

เที่ยว   tîiaao *(to travel, a trip, a pleasure tour)*

พวกเรากำลังไปเที่ยวเชียงใหม่

We are going on a trip to Chiangmai.

Example 4 – เปลี่ยน

Here we can see we have two consonants written together. Hopefully consonant clusters springs automatically to mind now; also, in this example, we have tone mark Mái èek:

/bpl/ + /iia/ + /n/ = /bpliian/

Tone Mark

Middle Class + Mái èek = *low tone*

เปลี่ยน = bpliian *(to change, to replace, to convert, to alter, to swap, to substitute, to transplant)*

Sample Sentence

ฉันเปลี่ยนใจไม่ไปภูเก็ตแล้ว

I have changed my mind not to go to Phuket.

Example 5 – เลี้ยง

Nothing difficult here as we swap consonants and the tone mark to give us:

/l/ + /iia/ + /ng/ = /liiang/

Tone Mark

Low Class + Mái too = *high tone*

เลี้ยง = líiang *(to feed, to nourish, to raise a child or animal, to provide for, to rear, to bring up, to foster, to nurse, to have a banquet, to hold a party, to feast)*

Sample Sentence

ฉันเลี้ยงหลานสาวสองคนตั้งแต่พวกเขาเกิด

- หลานสาว - *niece*

  I have brought my two nieces up since they were born.

Example 6 – เสีย

The initial consonant is now High Class, which gives us:

$$/s/ + /iia/ = /siia/$$

Tone Rules

High Class + Live syllable = *rising tone* (**HLR**)

เสีย = sĭia *(spent, broken, wasted, malfunctioning, defective, out of order, rotten, bad)*

<u>Sample Sentence</u>

รถของฉันเสีย

My car is broken down.

Two Syllables/Words

- เสียใจ

- เรียบร้อย

- เลี้ยวขวา

Example 8 – เสียใจ

We can see two separate vowels clearly: the vowel for this chapter is the first syllable, and a vowel which is always written before an initial consonant clearly marks the beginning of the second syllable/word. We covered the first syllable/word in the last example, so we now have:

เสีย + /j/ + /ai/ = เสีย-/**jai**/

Tone Rules

- Syllable 2: **M**iddle Class + **L**ive syllable = *mid tone* (**MLM**)

เสียใจ = sĭia-jai *(sorry)*

<u>Sample Sentence</u>

ฉันเสียใจด้วยนะที่คุณไม่ได้ชนะการแข่งขันนี้

- แข่งขัน - *to race, to contest, to compete*

    I'm sorry that you didn't win this contest.

Example 9 – เรียบร้อย

Naturally, with any unfamiliar words we find the written vowels.

With this example, the difficult part concerns the บ and the second ร, what are they doing?

Is บ a terminal consonant of the first syllable/word (เรียบ-); or, is บ the initial consonant of the second syllable word (-บร้อย) and there is either an unwritten vowel (/ɔɔ/) between it and the initial consonant of the third syllable (-บอ-ร้อย); or, do บ and ร form consonant clusters (-บร้อย)?

Well, the first clue is the tone mark. We know tone marks are written above an initial consonant and if there is a consonant cluster, then a tone mark is always written above the second consonant in the cluster. The question is, do บ and ร form consonant clusters?

No, they don't.

Consonant Clusters
begin with

ก, ข, ค, ต,

ป, ผ, *or* พ.

*The second conso-nant is **always***
ร, ล, *or* ว.

Table 3 on page 16 shows us that though ป can be an initial consonant in a consonant cluster, บ never is. Therefore, as บ and ร don't form consonant clusters, and the tone mark has to be written over an initial consonant, we deduce that บ does not belong to the syllable beginning with ร เรือ.

Therefore, it's either the initial consonant of the second syllable in a 3-syllable word (and there will be an unwritten /a/ between it and ร), or it is actually the final consonant of the 1st syllable (and there are only 2 syllables in this word). Which is it?

Unfortunately, there are no further clues to help us, so you either have to look-up the word, work it out from other context clues, or ask a friend. As it turns out, บ is the final consonant of the first syllable/word.

As we've already established that ร is the initial consonant of the second syllable/word (ร้อย), we now look at this and have to work out what อ is doing; is it a consonant or is it a vowel?

We've covered this combination many times before and this syllable/word follows the exact same pattern here, อ is the vowel สระ -อ. This gives us:

/r/ + /iia/ + /p/ - /r/ + /ɔɔ/ + /i/ = /riiap/-/rɔɔi/

Tone Rules

- Syllable 1: **L**ow Class + **D**ead syllable and **L**ong vowel = *falling tone* (**LDLF**)
- Syllable 2: Low Class + Mái too = *high tone*

เรียบร้อย = rîiap-rɔ́ɔi (*polite and well mannered*)

<u>*Sample Sentence*</u>

เขาเป็นเด็กผู้หญิงที่เรียบร้อยมาก

She is a very well-mannered girl.

Example 10 – เลี้ยวขวา

We can clearly see our vowel สระ เ-ีย and consonant ล ลิง, they make the **/liia/** sound. The next consonant is ว; is this the final consonant of the first syllable/word, an initial consonant of a syllable, or part of a consonant cluster? What comes after it?

Well, ข comes immediately after it, so ว and ข could form their own syllable; but, if we look at the consonant after the ข, we also see another ว. Does this have any bearing on what is happening here?

With any new word like this, once you've identified the vowels, always look to see if there is a consonant cluster, it's the next step in helping you work out what's going on.

As it turns out, though ว and ข don't form clusters, ข and ว do (Table 4). Now we know this, we're now only dealing with 2 consonants: '-ว' and 'ขว-'.

Therefore, the first ว is either the final consonant of the first syllable/word (**เลี้ยว**ขวา), or there has to be an unwritten vowel (**/a/**) between it and the consonant cluster ขว- (เลี้ย-วะ-ขวา). We hope you can follow the logic here!

Unfortunately, and as happens frequently, we're now at the point where we can't break this down any further and we need to use external means to solve it. After looking it up in the dictionary, we see that similar to ∪ in example 9, ว is the final consonant of the first syllable/word (where it makes the /o/ sound):

$$/l/ + /iia/ + /o/ + /kw/ + /aa/ = /liaao/-/kwaa/$$

You will encounter Low Class ว as the final consonant quite frequently and will get a feel for the words and their endings as your vocabulary and familiarity improve. It all comes down to practice.

Tone Rules

- Syllable 1: Low Class + Mái too = *high tone*
- Syllable 2: High Class + Live syllable = *rising tone* (**HLR**)

เลี้ยวขวา = líiao kwǎa *(turn right)*

<u>*Sample Sentence*</u>

กรุณาเลี้ยวขวาที่นั่นค่ะ

Please turn right over there.

Exercise 17

Exercise 17a

Answers begin on page 351

Match the words to their meaning:

1.	เรียบร้อย	to make an appointment with	a.
2.	เลี้ยวขวา	Phuket	b.
3.	เที่ยง	2, two	c.
4.	เปลี่ยน	to buy	d.
5.	เสียใจ	to turn right	e.
6.	ภูเก็ต	noon, 1200 hours	f.
7.	ที่นั่น	there, that place	g.
8.	เมียของเขา	polite, well-mannered	h.
9.	ไม่ได้	Chiang Mai	i.
10.	นัดพบ	his wife (informal)	j.
11.	เสีย	to change, to replace, to convert	k.
12.	สอง	didn't, did not, can't, cannot	l.
13.	ซื้อ	sorry	m.
14.	เกิด	spent, broken, bad, malfunction-ing	n
15.	เชียงใหม่	born, to happen, to take place	o

Exercise 17b

Identify the syllables in these words (draw a vertical line, underline, or highlight the syllables). Note, they are ordered by number of syllables, not necessarily complexity.

1. ตะเกียง   4. เกียจคร้าน   7. นักเรียนประถม

2. เลี้ยวซ้าย   5. เกี่ยวข้อง   8. โต๊ะเขียนหนังสือ

3. เทียบเคียง   6. เพียงอย่างเดียว   9. กระดาษเขียนหนังสือ

Their meaning:

1. ตะเกียง – *oil lamp*

2. เลี้ยวซ้าย – *to turn left*

3. เทียบเคียง – *to compare with*

4. เกียจคร้าน – *lazy*

5. เกี่ยวข้อง – *involve, concern*

6. เพียงอย่างเดียว – *single, sole, only*

7. นักเรียนประถม – *elementary student*

8. โต๊ะเขียนหนังสือ – *writing table/desk*

9. กระดาษเขียนหนังสือ – *writing paper.*

สระ เ-ือะ and สระ เ-ือ

สระ เ-ือะ makes the /ɯa/ as in *newer* sound, and สระ เ-ือ makes the /ɯɯa/ as in *skua* sound.

These sounds are the most difficult of the Thai sounds for non-natives to get right so you'll probably need to listen to a Thai native speaker to help.

We do have the full list of sounds in the *Learn Thai Alphabet application* if you want to take your learning to the next level and ensure perfection (www.learnthaialphabet.com).

The short vowel สระ เ-ือะ is <u>very rare</u>.

How are they used?

The long vowel เ-ือ is a vowel that is commonly seen and its format is easy to identify.

One Syllable Words

- เรือ
- เนื้อ
- เชื่อ

- เพื่อน
- เมือง

- เหมือน
- เครื่อง
- เดือน

Example 1 – เรือ

Our first example is very easy:

$$\text{/r/} + \text{/ɯɯa/} = \text{/rɯɯa/}$$

Tone Rules

Low Class + **L**ive syllable = *mid tone* (**LLM**)

เรือ = rɯɯa *(boat, ship, barge, vessel)*

<u>Sample Sentence</u>

ฉันเคยนั่งเรือเที่ยวในกรุงเทพ

I used to take boat trips in Bangkok.

Example 2 – เนื้อ

So is example 2:

$$\text{/n/} + \text{/ɯɯa/} = \text{/nɯɯa/}$$

Tone Mark

Low Class + Mái too = *high tone*

เนื้อ = nɯ́ɯa *(beef, meat of any animal, meat of the cow)*

<u>Sample Sentence</u>

ผมไม่ทานเนื้อ

I don't eat beef.

Example 3 – เชื่อ

A slight change, with a different consonant and Mái èek:

/ch/ + /ɰɰa/ = /chɰɰa/

Tone Mark

Low Class + Mái èek = *falling tone*

เชื่อ = chûɰa *(to believe, to trust, to have faith in, to rely on)*

Sample Sentence

ฉันเชื่อว่าคุณพูดความจริง

I believe that you speak the truth.

Example 4 – เพื่อน

We change the initial consonant and add a final consonant to give:

/p/ + /ɰɰa/ + /n/ = /pɰɰan/

Tone Mark

Low Class + Mái èek = *falling tone*

เพื่อน = pûɰan *(friend, pal, chum, buddy)*

Sample Sentence

คุณควรจะอยู่กับเพื่อนของคุณนะ

• ควรจะ - *should, ought to*

You should be with your friend.

Example 5 – เมือง

Again, there shouldn't be anything difficult with this word:

/m/ + /ɯɯa/ + /ng/ = /mɯɯang/

Tone Rules

Low Class + Live syllable = *mid tone* (**LLM**)

เมือง = mɯɯang (*city, nation, country, land, town*)

Sample Sentence

พวกเราจะไปในเมืองคืนนี้

We're going to the city tonight.

Example 6 – เหมือน

In this example we have High Class ห followed immediately by a familiar
Low Class consonant; and, as ม is a *single sound consonant*, High Class ห
is silent:

/**silent**/ + /m/ + /ɯɯa/ + /n/ = /mɯɯan/

Tone Rules

High Class + Live syllable = *rising tone* (**HLR**)

เหมือน = mɯ̌ɯan (*similar, all the same, like, as*)

Sample Sentence

บ้านหลังนี้เหมือนกับบ้านหลังนั้น

This house is similar to that one.

Example 7 – เครื่อง

We can see the tone mark written above the 2nd consonant, but once again we need to work out whether these 2 consonants form a consonant cluster or whether there are 2 separate syllables here.

As it turns out, ค and ร do form consonant clusters's and knowing this and the vowel shape makes this word easy:

/kr/ + /ɯɯa/ + /ng/ = /krɯɯang/

Tone Mark

Low Class + Mái èek = *falling tone*

เครื่อง = krɯ̂ɯang *(machine, apparatus, engine, mechanical device; classifier for engine)*

Sample Sentence

เครื่องยนต์นี้ทำงานผิดปกติ

This engine doesn't work properly.

Example 8 – เดือน

For our last single syllable word, we have:

/d/ + /ɯɯa/ + /n/ = /dɯɯan/

Tone Rules

Middle Class + Live syllable = *mid tone* (**MLM**)

เดือน = dɯɯan *(month)*

<u>*Sample Sentence*</u>

เทศกาลสงกรานต์อยู่ในเดือนเมษายน

- เทศกาลสงกราน - *Songkran festival*

- เมษายน - *April*

Songkran festival is in April.

Two Syllables/Words

- เมื่อไร
- เอื้อเฟื้อ

Example 9 – เมื่อไร

Looking for the vowels, we clearly see ไ-, which identifies the beginning of the second syllable:

/m/ + /ꞟꞟa/ + /r/ + /ai/ = /mꞟꞟa/-/rai/

Tone Rules

- Syllable 1: Low Class + Mái èek = *falling tone*
- Syllable 2: **Low Class** + **Live** syllable = *mid tone* (**LLM**)

เมื่อไร = mꞟꞟa-rai (*when?*)

<u>*Sample Sentence*</u>

คุณซื้อรถเมื่อไร

When did you buy the car?

Example 10 – เอื้อเฟื้อ

In our final example of this chapter, we have a repeated vowel. In the first syllable/word, we see the consonant อ อ่าง acting as a vowel placement consonant.

The second syllable/word is easy (/**f**/ as in **f**inished **p**icking):

/**silent**/ + /ʉʉa/ + /**f**/ + /ʉʉa/ = /**ʉʉa**/-/fʉʉa/

Tone Rules

Both syllables have the same tone marks:

- Syllable 1: Middle Class + Mái too = *falling tone*
- Syllable 2: Low Class + Mái too = *high tone*

เอื้อเฟื้อ = ʉ̂ʉa-fʉ́ʉa *(considerate, helpful, generous, friendly)*

<u>Sample Sentence</u>

เขาเป็นคนที่เอื้อเฟื้อมาก

He is a very generous person.

Real-life text

We're now over 90% of the way through the book and I hope you've got a feel for the way Thai script is written; and, perhaps contrary to what may have been your initial belief, it isn't as hard to read as you thought. We hope you're at the stage where you feel confident to start learning the actual consonant names as the names we use are there to get you up to speed quickly; and, eventually it's wise to learn the proper names. Don't worry if you haven't started learning them yet, but we do recommend you starting soon to complete your learning of the alphabet. Also, when you're progressing to writing Thai and need to ask someone how to spell a word, they can tell you the correct consonant and you can then impress them as you write it down.

Exercise 18

Exercise 18a

Answers begin on page 351

Match the words to their meaning:

1.	เครื่อง	city, nation, country, land, town	a.
2.	เรือ	to believe, to trust, to have faith in	b.
3.	เมษายน	boat, ship, barge, vessel	c.
4.	เดือน	machine, apparatus, engine, etc.	d.
5.	เทศกาลสงกรานต์	considerate, helpful, generous, friendly	e.
6.	เมื่อไร	to work, to do work	f.
7.	เนื้อ	month	g.
8.	เชื่อ	Songkran festival	h.
9.	เพื่อน	when?	i.
10.	ทำงาน	friend, buddy, chum	j.
11.	เมือง	beef, meat of any animal	k.
12.	เอื้อเฟื้อ	similar, like, as, all the same	l.
13.	พวกเรา	month of April	m.
14.	จะไป	generous, considerate, helpful	n
15.	เหมือน	will go	o

Exercise 18b

Identify the syllables in these words (draw a vertical line, underline, or highlight the syllables):

1. เกือบจะ   4. เคืองใจ   7. เนื่องมาจาก

2. เครือข่าย   5. พ่อเมือง   8. เพื่อนร่วมงาน

3. เดือนก่อน   6. เตือนสติ   9. สำนักงานตรวจคนเข้าเมือง

Their meanings are:

1. เกือบจะ – *about, almost, shortly*

2. เครือข่าย – *network, system*

3. เดือนก่อน – *last month*

4. เคืองใจ – *irritated, moody*

5. พ่อเมือง – *governor*

6. เตือนสติ – *to warn, to exhort, to admonish*

7. เนื่องมาจาก – *owing to, because, due to*

8. เพื่อนร่วมงาน – *colleague, co-worker, associate*

9. สำนักงานตรวจคนเข้าเมือง – *immigration bureau.*

สระ -ัวะ and สระ -ัว

The short vowel สระ -ัวะ is the last of the 4 rare vowels in Thai and it is unlikely that you will ever encounter any words that use it; however, สระ -ัว is very common.

สระ -ัวะ makes the **/ua/** as in *buat* sound and สระ -อัว makes the **/uua/** as in *pure* [gold] sound.

How are they used?

You can see that สระ -ะ is the distinguishing feature between them and, as we have seen many times before, it shortens the long vowel.

If you remember back to the chapter on สระ -ะ and Mái Hăn-aa-gàat (page 67), when written as a medial vowel, สระ -ะ becomes ไม้หันอากาศ (อ-).

However, though สระ -ัว is always written after an initial consonant, it can also have a final consonant itself (สระ -ัว-). When this occurs, ไม้หันอากาศ is omitted from -ัว- and it becomes -ว-. For example, with the word ขวด, the center character is not the Low Class consonant ว แหวน (Wɔɔ Wɛɛn) it is สระ -ัว with ไม้หันอากาศ omitted (-ว-).

One Syllable Words

- กลัว
- ขวด
- ช่วย
- ด้วย

- ตัว
- ถั่ว
- สวน

Note: *from hereon, we will refer to the Thai characters in their full Thai form, e.g. when we see ก we will refer to its proper name ก ไก่. This is the correct way to refer to the Thai consonants and is something you should try and learn.*

In the meantime, if you need to check out the transliterated names, you can do so on page 328 (you could also try transcribing them from the Thai if you need to practice).

Example 1 - กลัว

For our first example, we can quite clearly see the ก ไก่ and ล ลิง consonant cluster, and the long vowel:

$$/gl/ + /uua/ = /gluua/$$

Tone Mark

Middle Class + Live Syllable = *mid tone* (MLM)

กลัว = gluua *(afraid (of), scared, frightened)*

Sample Sentence

ฉันกลัวผู้ชายคนนั้น

I'm scared of that man.

Example 2 – ขวด

Here we have the example we mentioned earlier: ข ขวด, สระ –ัว, and ด
เด็ก:

$$/k/ + /uua/ + /t/ = /kuuat/$$

Tone Mark

High Class + Dead syllable = *low tone* (HDL)

ขวด = kùuat (classifier for *bottle*)

<u>*Sample Sentence*</u>

เอาน้ำเปล่าหนึ่งขวดครับ

I would like a bottle of water please.

Example 3 – ช่วย

A similar example with สระ –ัว as the medial vowel, ช ช้าง and ย ยักษ์ as
the initial and final consonants, respectively, and tone mark ไม้เอก gives us:

$$/ch/ + /uua/ + /i/ = /chuuai/$$

Tone Mark

Low Class consonant + ไม้เอก = *falling tone*

ช่วย = chûuai *(to help, to aid, to assist,
to contribute, to please)*

คุณต้องการความช่วยเหลือไหม

Do you need help?

Example 4 – ด้วย

Example 4 is straightforward with ด เด็ก, สระ -ัว, and ย ยักษ์:

/d/ + /uua/ + /i/ = /duuai/

Tone Mark

Middle Class + ไม้โท = _falling tone_

ด้วย = dûuai _(together, along with, also, too, as well, likewise)_

เราไปซื้อของด้วยกันไหม

Shall we go shopping together?

Example 5 – ตัว

We have ต เต่า as an initial consonant; but without a final consonant, ไม้หันอากาศ must always be written:

/dt/ + /uua/ = /dtuua/

Tone Mark

Middle Class + Live syllable = _mid tone_ (MLM)

ตัว = dtuua *(self, himself, herself, yourself,*
themselves, body, classifier for animals)

Sample Sentence

ดูแลตัวเองด้วยนะ

Look after yourself.

Example 6 – ถั่ว

Here we see the initial consonant is now High Class ถ ถุง with the addition
of ไม้เอก:

$$/t/ + /uua/ = /tuua/$$

Tone Mark

High Class + ไม้เอก = *low tone*

ถั่ว = tùua *(bean, green bean)*

Sample Sentence

เขาชอบทานถั่วฝักยาว
He likes eating green beans.

Example 7 – สวน

Switching back to our vowel in the medial position, we have ส เสือ and น
หนู as the initial and final consonants:

$$/s/ + /uua/ + /n/ = /suuan/$$

Tone Mark

High Class + Live syllable = *rising tone*

สวน = sǔuan *(garden, field, park, farm)*

Sample Sentence

ไปเดินเล่นที่สวนสาธารณะกันเถอะ

Let's take a walk in the park.

Two Syllables/Words

- ครอบครัว
- ชั่วโมง
- ตัวอย่าง

Example 8 – ครอบครัว

With our first two syllable/word example, we can see the second syllable/word is comprised of the consonant cluster ค ควาย, ร เรือ (คร) and สระ ◌ัว; this just leaves us ครอบ. This syllable/word begins with exactly the same consonant cluster, followed by สระ -อ as our written vowel, and บ ใบไม้ as the final consonant.

/kr/ + /ɔɔ/ + /p/ + /kr/ + /uua/ = /krɔɔp/-/kruua/

Tone Mark

- Syllable 1: Low Class + Dead syllable + Long Vowel = *falling tone* (LDLF)
- Syllable 2: Low Class + Long Vowel = *mid tone* (LLM)

ครอบครัว = krɔ̂ɔp- kruua *(family)*

ครอบครัวของฉันอยู่ที่จังหวัดสุรินทร์

My family lives in Surin province.

Example 9 – ชั่วโมง

The two written vowels clearly identify the two syllable/words here. We've encountered the second syllable/word before and neither it, nor the first part should pose any problems.

The first syllable is made up of ช ช้าง, สระ ˘ัว, and ไม้เอก; and the second syllable of ม ม้า, สระ โ-, and ง งู:

/ch/ + /uua/ + /m/ + /oo/ + /ng/ = /chuua/-/moong/

Tone Mark

- Syllable 1: Low Class + ไม้เอก = _falling tone_
- Syllable 2: Low Class + Live syllable = _mid tone_ (LLM)

ชั่วโมง = chûua-moong _(hour)_

จากกรุงเทพไปสุรินทร์ ใช้เวลาเดินทางประมาณ 6 ชั่วโมง

It takes about six hours to travel from Bangkok to Surin.

Example 10 – ตัวอย่าง

This last example is slightly different to those encountered previously; but, first, we'll run through their make-up: in the first syllable we have ต เต่า and

สระ ◌ัว; and, in the second syllable we have: อ อ่าง, ย ยักษ์, ไม้เอก, สระ -า, and ง งู.

Though we haven't covered the second syllable/word yet, we have seen อ being used as a preceding consonant many times before. You may also recall that we mentioned there are only 4 words in the Thai lexicon to which อ acts in this capacity; and, this is one of them (the remainder can be found in Appendix F on page 337). So, knowing that, we have:

/dt/ + /uua/ + /silent/ + /y/ + /aa/ + /ng/ = /dtuua/-/yaang/

Tone Rules

- Syllable 1: Middle Class + Live syllable = *mid tone* (MLM)
- Syllable 2: Middle Class + ไม้เอก = *low tone*

ตัวอย่าง = dtuaa-yàang *(example, sample)*

Sample Sentence

นี่คือสินค้าตัวอย่าง

This is a sample product.

Exercise 19

Exercise 19a

Answers begin on page 352

Match the words to their meaning:

1.	ครอบครัวของฉัน	to want, to need, to require	a.
2.	ช่วย	example, sample	b.
3.	เดิน	to help, to aid, to assist, to contribute	c.
4.	น้ำเปล่า	my family	d.
5.	สวน	drinking water	e.
6.	กลัว	to walk	f.
7.	ตัว	park, farm, field, park	g.
8.	ต้องการ	one bottle of water	h.
9.	จากกรุงเทพไปสุรินทร์	6 hours	i.
10.	ด้วย	from Bangkok to Surin	j.
11.	ตัวอย่าง	scared, afraid of	k.
12.	ถั่วฝักยาว	cow peas (green beans)	l.
13.	6 ชั่วโมง	Surin province	m.
14.	น้ำเปล่าหนึ่งขวด	together, along with, also, too	n
15.	จังหวัดสุรินทร์	body, him/herself, themselves	o

Exercise 19b

Identify the syllables in these words (draw a vertical line, underline, or high-light the syllables):

1. กระทรวง   4. จำนวน   7. ควรปฏิบัติ

2. ต้นมะม่วง   5. ชนวน   8. ดวงวิญญาณ

3. ขวดนม   6. ช่วยงาน   9. ปวงชนชาวไทย

Their meanings are:

1. กระทรวง – *ministry*

2. ต้นมะม่วง – *mango tree*

3. ขวดนม – *milk bottle*

4. จำนวน – *amount*

5. ชนวน – *fuse, primer*

6. ช่วยงาน – *to help, support*

7. ควรปฏิบัติ – *should follow*

8. ดวงวิญญาณ – *soul*

9. ปวงชนชาวไทย – *Thai population.*

Notes

ฤ and ฤๅ

The vowels in this chapter are สระ ฤ, which makes the /**rʉ**/ as in **roo**k sound; and, สระ ฤๅ, which makes the /**rʉʉ**/ as in **roo**t sound. These are not particularly common vowels but you should have no trouble identifying them.

How are they used?

As we've repeatedly emphasised all along, Thai vowels always make the same sound regardless of the consonants they are written with; however, you've perhaps already realised that the initial sound of the vowels in this section are **actually a consonant sound**: the /r/ sound. After diligently working this far through the book, we know that the only consonant in the Thai alphabet that makes the /r/ sound is ร; and, ร เรือ is a Low Class consonant.

Different Vowel Sounds

Okay, we did tell you a little white lie before (sorry about that, but we did wait until page 291 of the book before we revealed our dishonesty) but these vowels are slightly different in that the short vowel can make 3 different sounds depending on its position in the word (this is the only vowel that makes a different sound). The rules for this are:

> 1. ฤ (/**rʉ**/) is pronounced /**ri**/ when it follows ก, ต, ท, ป, ศ, or ส. For exam-
>
>   ple, with the word กฤช, it is pronounced /**grĭt**/ (*dagger*).

---

2. ฤ (/rʉ/) is pronounced /rʉ/ when it follows ค, น, พ, ม, or ห. For example, with the word ประพฤติ, which is pronounced /bprà-prʉt/ *(to behave, to act, to perform or do manner.*

3. ฤ (/rʉ/) is pronounced /rəə/ in the word ฤกษ์, (/rɘ̂ɘk/) which means *auspicious occasion, auspicious time.* This is the only word in which this pronunciation is found.

Rule 1 still applies here as this vowel begins with the consonant 'r' sound.

One Syllable Words

- ฤกษ์
- ฤทธิ์
- กฤช

Example 1 – ฤกษ์

Here we have the short vowel ฤ, plus ก ไก่, ษ ฤๅษี, and the การันต์. This gives us:

$$/rəə/ + /k/ + /silent/ = /rəək/$$

Tone Rules

As we said in the 'How are they used?' paragraph, this vowel makes the /r/ sound, which is a Low Class consonant sound:

Low Class + Dead syllable + Long Vowel = *falling tone* (LDLF)

ฤกษ์ = rɘ̂ɘk *(auspicious occasion, auspicious time)*

นี่เป็นฤกษ์ดีสำหรับงานแต่งงาน

This is an auspicious time for a wedding.

Example 2– ฤทธิ์

As the short vowel ฤ precedes the Low Class consonant ท ทหาร it makes

the /**ri**/ sound. We also have ธ ธง, สระ ◌ิ, and the การันต์

/ri/ + /t/ + /silent/ = /rit/

Tone Rules

Low Class + Dead syllable + Short Vowel = _high tone_ (LDSH)

ฤทธิ์ = rít _(effect, supernatural power)_

ยานี้ออกฤทธิ์เร็วมาก

This pill will take effect quickly.

Example 3 – กฤช

Here we see the short vowel ฤ written after ก ไก่; and, we have ช ช้าง as
the final consonant:

/g/ + /ri/ + /t/

Tone Rules

Middle Class + Dead syllable = _low tone_ (MDL)

กฤช = grìt _(dagger)_

เขาซื้อกฤชทองเล่มนี้มาจากร้านขายของเก่า

He bought the gold dagger from an antique shop.

Two Syllables/Words

- อังกฤษ

- ประพฤติ

- ฤดู

- ฤๅษี

Example 4 - อังกฤษ

A very common word and it consists of two syllables. The first syllable has: อ อ่าง, ไม้หันอากาศ, and ง งู; the second syllable has: ก ไก่, the vowel, and ษ ฤๅษี. อ is acting as a vowel placement consonant here.

$$/silent/ + /a/ + /ng/ - /g/ + /rì/ + /t/ = /ang/-/grìt/$$

Tone Rules

Syllable 1: Middle Class + Live syllable = *mid tone* (MLM)

Syllable 2: Middle Class + Dead syllable = *low tone* (MDL)

อังกฤษ = ang-grìt *(England, English, Great Britain, British)*

เขาเป็นคนอังกฤษ

He is English.

Example 5 - ประพฤติ

In this two syllable word, we see สระ -ะ and know that this always marks the end of a syllable or word; and, therefore, Low Class พ พาน must be the initial consonant of the second syllable. Looking at the two consonants at the start of the word (ป ปลา and ร เรือ) we've seen this combination before and know they form a common consonant cluster. Therefore, the first syllable is:

$$\text{/bpr/ + /a/ = /bpra/}$$

In the second syllable we have: พ พาน; the vowel ฤ; and, at the very end, you see ติ (ต เต่า and สระ -ิ). Logic tells us that this should make the /dt/ + /i/ sound, but this is actually incorrect. Though the consonant is actually the terminal consonant of the second syllable - and is spoken in this word - the short vowel above it isn't.

$$\text{/p/ + /rʉ/ + t/ = /prʉt/}$$

Together they form:

$$\text{/bpra/ + /prʉt/ = /bpra/-/prʉt/}$$

Tone Rules

- Syllable 1: Middle Class + Dead syllable = *low tone* (MDL)
- Syllable 2: Low Class + Dead syllable and Short Vowel = *high tone* (LDSH)

ประพฤติ = bprà-prʉ́t *(to behave, to act, to perform)*

Sample Sentence

วันนี้เขาประพฤติแย่มาก

He behaved badly today.

Example 6 - ฤดู

For the last short vowel example, we see the vowel forms the first syllable, and we have Middle Class ด เด็ก and สระ ◌ู in the second syllable:

$$/rɨ/ + /d/ + /uu/ = /rɨ/-/duu/$$

Tone Rules

- Syllable 1: Low Class + Dead syllable and Short Vowel = *high tone* (LDSH)

- Syllable 2: Middle Class + Live syllable = *mid tone* (MLM)

ฤดู = rɨ́-duu (*season, period*)

เมืองไทยมี 3 ฤดู

There are three seasons in Thailand.

Example 7 - ฤๅษี

In the last example of the book we see the long vowel สระ ฤๅ (which is a syllable in it's own right) and the long สระ ◌ี written above High Class ษ ฤๅษี. As vowels are written above initial consonants, we know that this has to be start of the second syllable. We have:

$$/rɨɨ/ + /s/ + /ii/ = /rɨɨ/-/sii/$$

Tone Rules

- Syllable 1: Low Class + Live syllable = *mid tone* (LLM)
- Syllable 2: High Class + Live syllable = *rising tone* (HLR)

ฤๅษี = rɨɨ-sǐi (*hermit, anchorite, ascetic*)

<u>*Sample Sentence*</u>

ฤๅษีเป็นคนที่มีพลังพิเศษ

The hermit is a powerful man.

ฤๅ and ฦๅ

Though there used to be a few words in the Thai language that used these vowels, they are all now obsolete and you won't find them anywhere in modern language.

Reading Strategies and Texts

Reading Strategies

If you don't know anything about reading strategies, then this section will be particularly applicable to you.

Using the analogy of a painter staring at a blank canvas and not knowing where to begin, even unsure of how or where to paint the first brush stroke, is comparable to a novice reader trying to learn a new language, being given a multi-page book and told to *'get on with it'*.

Okay, you can open the book and turn to the first page, but then what?

Maybe you manage to get past that dread feeling of seeing a mass of unfamiliar text on the first page. Perhaps you even have the motivation and will to overcome the hypnotising and demoralising effect this unfamiliar script has on you and manage to mobilise yourself into starting at the very first word of the very first sentence.

The problem is, if you then go through it slowly, reading word by word, there is a high possibility that it will take you a long time. What's more, and this is an educated guess, you will probably get bored fairly quickly and possibly even lose interest. Let's face it, it's just not an effective approach to reading (any kind of reading, let alone reading an unfamiliar language). No, there is a better way, a far better way with a greater chance of success than being thrown in at the deep end and told to sink-or-swim, That way is to use reading strategies.

Even if you've never heard of these, or don't specifically know what reading strategies or their names are, I'm sure you'll be familiar with some of them.

Scanning

For example, imagine you're going on a journey and need to find out what time your train or plane leaves. The first thing you'll do is grab a timetable, flick your eyes quickly over the letters, the numbers (be it on a monitor, on your tablet, smartphone, sign, or even a sheet of paper) and try and find the specific bits of information that you need. You're ignoring practically everything else, just searching for the info you need. This technique – *this strategy* – is called **scanning:** you scan a piece of text quickly for the information you need. It is a very effective tool for identifying specific terms of words, or pieces of information that you require and we can use this effectively with reading Thai. We'll come onto more about this in a moment.

Skimming

For our next strategy, if you go to the table of contents of this or any book, you will see sections, chapters, main headings, sub-headings, and so on. Using this contents list, you can quickly scan it to find the topic that interests you, and then go straight to that page. Then, when you're on the page that you want, there may even be more sub-levels of headings or bullet points to flick through to find the information you need.

Once you find the part you think contains the information you need, you can quickly read the first sentence or the paragraph to find out what the sentence or paragraph is about. You don't read every word, you just **skim** over it to find out (quickly) the rough idea and to see if you need to spend more time on this part. If it isn't the information you need, you can keep searching, **skimming** quickly over the text until you locate the precise information you're looking for. Used in conjunction with *scanning*, **skimming** is another very effective reading strategy.

How Do We Apply This To Our Thai Reading?

As a beginner, you need to learn vocabulary. That part of it is both simple and obvious. You're new to reading Thai and the chances are you probably know very little, or even next to nothing, and you know you can't progress significantly without it.

You will find it enormously frustrating to read texts at first as you quite simply don't know enough words; and, with most texts, the number of words you don't know far exceeds the ones you do. There isn't a way around this, you quite simply have to build your vocabulary if you're going to read.

Note: *if the material you're trying to read has more unknown words than known, then it's maybe a good idea to switch to slightly easier texts. It is easy to become frustrated and demotivated in the initial stages; and, let's face it, first-things first - don't start trying to sprint when you haven't even learnt to walk! Recommendations are that material should always be challenging: if it's too easy you will become bored, if it's too difficult it will be demotivating.*

However, once you have built-up your vocabulary, reading will become much easier: the *scanning* technique will be more useful to you at first, as you can scan the text to find words you know or even don't know. However, once you improve, *skimming* will then come in useful to identify the meaning of a sentence, or the main idea of the text. Ultimately, with both strategies, as your vocabulary range improves, the ratio of known-to-unknown words switches and then you will start to 'see' words on the page. Once you then become proficient, you can then use scanning and skimming to quickly go over a paragraph and identify the words that you're either unfamiliar with, or don't know (we imagine this is much the same as you do in your native tongue).

When reading texts for the first time, it's important not to get bogged-down by unfamiliar words. If you allow this to happen, you then end up reaching for the dictionary constantly and end up not reading Thai at all - you need to get away from doing this, and the next two strategies will help you with unfamiliar/unknown words.

Highlighting

All through your language learning, if you don't do this already, it may help to categorise 3 kinds of word: those you know, those you think you know, and those you don't know. You can label them: *1) known*, *2) unsure*, and 3) *unknown*.

When you start on a new text, we recommend *skimming* through the paragraph/page/chapter (depending on length) quickly skim reading and with your highlighter, underline any '*unsure*' or '*unknown*' word. This may take you a while at first, but the idea is you try and do this as quickly as you can and as you become more skilled, your speed and accuracy will improve.

After you've finished this skim/scan, you can then proceed to read the text in detail. What you're now trying to do is to read and understand each sentence. Then each paragraph. Then the chapter. Then the story.

As you move throught the text you will encounter the words you are either unsure about or don't know. Maybe you can modify your underlined choices from your detailed reading.

An *unsure* word will then either be marked as '*known*' or '*unknown*'. If it's *known* you can leave it, but if you can't work out the meaning, then it needs to be marked *unknown:* give it a **full-strike-through** with the highlighter (they're easier to see later for checking). Then, continue throughout the entire text until finished. Hopefully, you can grasp the overall meaning of what you've just read. Maybe at first it'll be 20%, or 40% of the text; but, if you carry on diligently, this will soon rise as you learn more words.

Now it's time to work out what the *unknown* words mean; but, <u>before you reach for the dictionary</u>, you may have changed some of your *unsure* words to *known* based on what you were reading.

Context Clues

As you read through the text, if you can't discern the meaning from the words you do know, then maybe the sub-heading, the heading, or even the title (if it's a short story) can provide you with a context of some kind (we all like to know what we're reading).

For example, in children's books, the pictures are not only there to provide colour or a break for the eyes, they also provide us with visual clues as to what's going on in the story at that time.

These, in conjunction with other words in the same or surrounding sentences may give you a clue as to the meaning of a highlighted *unknown* word. Verbs are particularly useful as they provide us with the 'action' in the story and a sentence is not a complete sentence unless it has a subject and a verb; so, if you can learn the verbs, you may be able to grasp the meaning of the sentence far more rapidly.

When word, pictures, tables, graphs, charts, and other objects are used in this manner we call them ***context clues***, as they give us a clue about the meaning of the text we're reading. They are very effective and will not only help you work out the meaning of the text, but will prevent you from having to reach for the dictionary every 5 seconds!

Sure, if you need the dictionary, use it; but, if you can hold off until the end, then do so: look-up all the unknown words at the same time as it'll speed up your use of the dictionary and ensure you don't get into the bad habit of using the dictionary every time you see a word you don't know.

Afterwards, see which ones you got right and which ones you didn't. Ask yourself why didn't you get them right as analysing your work in order to improve is also an effective learning strategy – be honest about it, we all have to begin somwhere.

Fluency

Also, when you've read a text, try and work out how much of it you actually comprehended. Only you can gauge whether you're comfortable or satisfied-with the level that you're at.

This satisfaction level will be different for you than it will be for others, as fluency means different things to different people. For example, some might be happy understanding the overall meaning of the passage (say 70-80%), whereas others want to get every word 100% correct. It all depends on what your actual reading goal and the reason for reading the text is.

Speaking personally, if I pick up a technical document (in English) I know there'll be words in their I'm unfamiliar with but I'll get most of them: I expect to understand at least 99%. However, if I pick up a medical paper, I'll be lucky if I know more than 60-70% of the words (the remainder will be the medical terms). I'm not concerned by this though as long as I achieve my particular goal for reading it.

For example, quite recently I had to write a research paper on how a knowledge of phonology can help victims of Aphasia. Though I have a certain knowledge of Aphasia, the medical terminolgy is lacking and is not something I'm particularly strong on. However, by using the four strategies just discussed, I could quickly and easily locate the exact information I wanted and finished the paper. I didn't need to read all my research, I didn't need to understand the medical terminolgy, I just needed a certain level of language ability to do it. I also used the four strategies above to the utmost and without them I'd have been floundering! It all depends on what you're reading, your reasons for reading it, and what you hope to achieve.

Top-down v Bottom-up Models

The methods we are talking about here are what are collectively called 'top-down' models (there are many more, but these 4 are a good start for you). We mentioned at the very beginning that the way we teach you in this book is very much a 'bottom-up' method: it's step-by-step, it's very detailed, but we can't really use any of our own knowledge with the language simply because we don't have that much of it.

However, you now have some knowledge of the language and the process for reading Thai script; and, you now know **exactly** what you have to to do to become a proficient, strategic reader. You now have to apply these theories and make them work for you; and, as you improve, you can (and will) start bringing your own life experiences and background knowledge to each subject.

So, by learning what you have in this book and by employing these simple every-day models, we hope that you will no longer look at that mass of text on the page, and think 'where do I start'. Instead, you'll get stuck right in, put your knowledge and models to good use, and find that as your Thai reading ability improves, your confidence, motivation, and self-efficacy will rise to match it.

Reading Thai Texts

In this section we're going to look at some reading passages. There are 6 passages in total, ranging from Prathomsuksa 1 (age 7 years) through to Prathomsuksa 6 (age 12 years); and we hope you can decipher and read these.

Having worked this far through the book, you are now equipped with all the skills and knowledge to be able to break down these individual sentences and paragraphs and read them end-to-end. However, what you must appreciate and understand is, at this stage, it's very unlikely that you will know the meaning of these texts – as we mentioned right back at the beginning of this book, this is pure and simply because you do not have sufficient vocabulary.

The good news is that doesn't actually matter as you now have the building blocks to address this: you have the skills to begin working through these and other real-life texts; and, you know you have the knowledge and ability to break sentences down into words, and words into syllables. Hopefully, apart from the occasional dip into it, transliterated text is now a thing of the past.

Yes, you will be a slow reader but show me a beginner who isn't. In your child-hood days you may have been one of the fortunate ones who never fell off their bike and scraped a knee when the stabilisers first came off, but I bet you a dime-to-a-dozen, you wavered, you stumbled, you took it steady, and through steadily building your skills, your ability and confidence grew over time until you can't even remember the problems you once had.

This is the same with any motor skill and though we would all like to hit the ground at 60 mph, in all honesty, it takes a little time and a lot of practice to be able to reach that level - reading is the same. So, take your time. Little and often is key to many things and learning to read and comprehend is one of those.

At the end of the book, you will also see some links to other resources on the Internet. We encourage you to use these when you have time as the more you read, the better you become.

You do have a unique advantage over many who visit the various websites and embark on these exercises, and that is you know far more than 99% of those who waste time searching for free material. The vast majority of these people are 'hoarders', they just store material on their computers in the hope that one day they might need it (and never view it again). However, now you've worked through this book, you have a sound knowledge of how the language and script ties together and this, together with your knowledge, your ability, and your drive will take you further on your own Quest than you ever thought possible.

Prathomsuksa 1

ครอบครัวของฉัน

ครอบครัวของฉัน มีสมาชิกอยู่หลายคน มีพ่อ แม่ พี่ น้อง ปู่ ย่า ตา ยาย
รวมกันเป็นครอบครัวใหญ่

ปู่ คือ พ่อของพ่อ ย่า คือ แม่ของพ่อ ตา คือ พ่อของแม่ ยาย คือ
แม่ของแม่

พี่ของฉัน ตัวฉัน และน้องของฉัน เป็นลูกของพ่อกับแม่

พ่อของฉันเป็นลูกของปู่กับย่า ส่วนแม่ของฉันเป็นลูกของตากับยาย

ฉันกับน้องๆ จึงเป็นหลานของปู่ ย่า ตา และยาย

ครอบครัวของฉัน มีพ่อและแม่เป็นหัวหน้าครอบครัว

พ่อและแม่คอยช่วยดูแลความเป็นอยู่ของพวกเราทุกคนในครอบครัว

Reference: มานพ สอนศิริ, รศ.ดร. สิริพัชร์ เจษฎาวิโรจน์, เฉลา อรุณรัตน์. ภาษาไทย
หลักภาษาและการใช้ภาษา ป.๑. กรุงเทพฯ : อักษรเจริญทัศน์ อจท. จำกัด, .. (หน้า 18)

Translation

My family

My family has many members: father, mother, older brother, younger brother and grandparents. We live together as a big family.

Grandfather (ปู่) is father's father. Grandmother (ย่า) is father's mother.

Grandfather (ตา) is mother's father. Grandmother (ยาย) is mother's mother.

My older brother, younger brother, and I are our parents' children. My father is grandparents' son. My mother is grandparents' daughter. My brothers and I are grandchildren.

My family has our father and mother as leaders. My father and mother take care of all of us in the family.

Prathomsuksa 2

คนดีมีน้ำใจ

เช้าวันเสาร์อากาศเย็นสบาย น้องแก้วตื่นแต่เช้า เก็บที่นอน อาบน้ำ

แต่งตัว แล้วรีบรับประทานอาหารเช้า

เพราะคุณพ่อและคุณแม่จะพาไปเที่ยวสวนสนุก

เมื่อไปถึงสวนสนุก น้องแก้วก็วิ่งไปที่เครื่องเล่นอย่างรวดเร็ว

'ระวังลูก อย่ารีบวิ่ง เดี๋ยวจะหกล้มนะจ๊ะ' คุณแม่บอกน้องแก้ว

น้องแก้วเล่นม้าหมุน ชิงช้าสวรรค์ และเครื่องเล่นอื่นๆ

อีกหลายอย่างจนเกือบเที่ยง

คุณพ่อและคุณแม่จึงพาน้องแก้วไปรับประทานอาหารที่ร้านค้าในสวนสนุก

Reference: วีณา วงศ์ศรีเผือก และคณะ. ภาษาไทย ป.๒. กรุงเทพฯ : อักษรเจริญทัศน์ อจท. จำกัด,
๒๕๕๒ (หน้า 14)

Translation

Good Persons

Saturday morning is nice and cool. Nong Kaew (Nɔ́ɔng Gɛ̂ɛo) woke up very early, made the bed, had a shower, got dressed, and had breakfast quickly because her parents were taking her to the amusement park.

When they arrived at the park, Nong Kaew (Nɔ́ɔng Gɛ̂ɛo) ran straight to the amusements.

"Be careful. Don't run. You might fall down", mother told Nong Kaew (Nɔ́ɔng Gɛ̂ɛo). Nong Kaew (Nɔ́ɔng Gɛ̂ɛo) enjoyed the merry go-around, the Ferris wheel, and the other amusements until almost noon. Her parents are taking her to have lunch at a food shop at the park.

Prathomsuksa 3

เพลงกล่อมเด็กของคุณแม่

แพรวาเป็นนักเรียนชั้น ป. ๓ ของโรงเรียนบ้านปันน้ำใจ

เมื่อถึงวันหยุดสุดสัปดาห์ แพรวาจะช่วยแม่ทำงานบ้าน และเลี้ยงน้อง

น้องพลอยใสน้องของแพรวาเพิ่งอายุได้ ๗ เดือน เท่านั้น

ซึ่งแพรวารักน้องของเธอมาก

วันเสาร์นี้ก็เช่นกัน แพรวาทำการบ้านเสร็จแล้วไปช่วยแม่ตากผ้า

จากนั้นเธออ่านหนังสือนิทานที่ขอยืมมาจากห้องสมุด

แม่อุ้มน้องพลอยใสไว้บนตัก แล้วร้องเพลงกล่อมน้องด้วยน้ำเสียงนุ่มนวล

ชวนฟัง แพรวานั่งอ่านหนังสืออยู่ไม่ไกลนักหยุดอ่าน

แล้วฟังแม่ร้องเพลงกล่อมเด็ก

Reference: มานพ สอนศิริ และคณะ. ภาษาไทย วรรณคดีและวรรณกรรม ป.๓. กรุงเทพฯ :

อักษรเจริญทัศน์ อจท. จำกัด, ... (หน้า 44)

Translation

Cradle Songs

Praewa (Prɛɛ-wa) is a student in grade 3 of Ban Pan Nam-jai (Bâan Pan Nám-jai) School. At the weekend, she helps her mother work in the house and takes care of her younger sister. Her sister, Ploysai (Plɔɔi-sǎi), is only 7 months old. Praewa (Prɛɛ-wa) loves her sister very much.

This Saturday, she finished her homework and then helped her mother to hang up the laundry. After that, she read the story she has borrowed from the library.

Mother held Ploysai (Plɔɔi-sǎi) on her lap and sang cradle songs for her gently and beautifully. Praewa (Prɛɛ-wa) was reading the story nearby, she then stopped reading and listened to her mother sang the cradle songs.

Prathomsuksa 4

สวัสดีวันเปิดเทอม

วันนี้เป็นวันเปิดเทอม เด็กๆ ดีใจที่ได้เรียนชั้นใหม่ ได้เจอเพื่อนใหม่และ
มีคุณครูประจำชั้นคนใหม่ด้วย

เด็ดเดี่ยวและไพลินมาถึงโรงเรียนแต่เช้า เด็กทั้งคู่เป็นเพื่อนสนิทกัน
เด็ดเดี่ยวเห็นไพลินกำลังทักทายเพื่อนใหม่
จึงเข้าไปทักทายเพื่อนใหม่บ้าง

เชิงขวัญบอกเด็ดเดี่ยวและไพลินว่า คุณพ่อของเธอเป็นตำรวจ
ตอนนี้คุณพ่อต้องย้ายเข้ามาทำงานที่กรุงเทพมหานคร
เธอจึงต้องย้ายโรงเรียนมาเรียนในกรุงเทพมหานครตามคุณพ่อด้วย

เมื่อพูดกันได้สักพัก ก็ถึงเวลาเข้าแถวเคารพธงชาติ
เมื่อเคารพธงชาติเสร็จเรียบร้อยแล้ว
นักเรียนแต่ละชั้นก็เดินแยกย้ายกันไป
เข้าห้องเรียนอย่างเป็นระเบียบเรียบร้อย

Reference: เอกรินทร์ สี่มหาศาล และคณะ. ภาษาไทย ป.๔, กรุงเทพฯ : อักษรเจริญทัศน์ อจท. จำกัด,
๒๕๕๓ (หน้า 9)

Translation

Welcome to the New Term

Today is the first day of the new term. The children are happy that they have moved up to another level. They have met new friends and also their new advisor.

Deddiaw (Dèt-diiao) and Pailin (Pai-lin) arrived at the school very early. They are close friends. Deddiaw (Dèt-diiao) saw Pailin greeting new friends, so he went to greet the new friends too.

Cherngkwan (Chəəng-kwǎn) told Deddiaw (Dèt-diiao) and Pailin (Pai-lin) that her father is a policeman. Her father has moved to work in Bangkok, so she had to move with her father to study in Bangkok.

The conversation has been going for a while; it is time for the morning activity to line up for the national anthem. When the activity is finished, the students walk to their classrooms nicely.

Prathomsuksa 5

นิทานพื้นบ้านไทย

'ปัญญา เธอช่วยแนะนำนิทานพื้นบ้านให้ฉันสักเรื่องได้ไหม' สันติขอร้อง

'ฉันจะต้องทำรายงานเรื่องนิทานพื้นบ้านส่งคุณครูสุพัตรา ทีนี้ฉันอยาก

ใส่ตัวอย่างนิทานพื้นบ้านประกอบเนื้อหารายวิชาน่ะ'

ปัญญาพยักหน้า แล้วตอบสันติว่า 'ฉันเคยอ่านนิทานพื้นบ้านหลายเรื่อง

เหมือนกัน บางทีแม่ก็เล่าให้ฉันฟังบ้าง ฉันเล่านิทานพื้นบ้านที่เคยอ่านมา

ให้เธอฟังก่อนดีไหม เผื่อเธอจะชอบ' 'ดีสิ ว่าแต่เธอจะเล่าเรื่องอะไรหรือ'

สันติถาม

'เรื่องพระเจ้าสายน้ำผึ้งและพระนางสร้อยดอกหมาก นิทานเรื่องนี้เป็น

นิทานพื้นบ้านของจังหวัดพระนครศรีอยุธยานะ' ปัญญาตอบแล้วเล่า

นิทานพื้นบ้านเรื่อง พระเจ้าสายน้ำผึ้งและพระนางสร้อยดอกหมาก

ให้สันติฟัง

Reference: ขัณธ์ชัย อธิเกียรติ, รศ.ดร. สิริพัชร์ เจษฎาวิโรจน์. ภาษาไทย วรรณคดีและวรรณกรรม ป.๕. กรุงเทพฯ : อักษรเจริญทัศน์ อจท. จำกัด, ... (หน้า 5)

Translation

Thai Traditional Tales

"Panya (Pan-ya), can you suggest any traditional tale for me?", Santi (Săn-tì) asked. "I have to do a report about it to submit to Miss Supattra (Su-pát-traa). So, I would like to add the sample of the story for the report."

Panya (Pan-ya) nodded and answered to Santi (Săn-tì), "I have read many stories and sometimes my mother told me some. I will tell you the one that I read and you might like it."

"Good. What is the name of the tale you are going to tell me?"

"It is *King Sai-nam-pueng* (Săi-nám-pûeng) and *Queen Soi-dok-mak* (Sôoi-dɔɔk-màak). This tale is a traditional tale of Ayutthaya province", Panya (Pan-ya) answered and told Santi (Săn-tì) the tale.

Prathomsuksa 6

จดแล้วจำ

เมื่อ ๒ สัปดาห์ที่ผ่านมา อานุช อาของสันตินำลูกแมวพันธุ์วิเชียรมาศ

ที่ได้จากเพื่อนคนหนึ่งมาให้พ่อของสันติช่วยเลี้ยงดู เนื่องจากอานุชย้าย

ที่ทำงานใหม่จึงต้องย้ายที่พักด้วย ที่พักใหม่ของอานุชเป็นห้องชุด

หรือที่เรียกว่าคอนโดมิเนียม จึงไม่สามารถเลี้ยงสัตว์ได้ เพราะสัตว์

ที่เลี้ยงอาจจะทำความรำคาญให้แก่ผู้พักอาศัยคนอื่นๆ ได้

สันติและอุษาตื่นเต้นมากที่จะมีสัตว์เลี้ยงเป็นของตัวเอง

พ่อแม่เห็นว่าการเลี้ยงสัตว์จะทำให้เด็กๆ มีจิตใจดี มีความเมตตากรุณา

และยังเป็นการฝึกให้มีความรับผิดชอบด้วย

จึงตกลงให้สันติและอุษาเลี้ยงลูกแมวที่อานุชให้มา

ลูกแมวน้อยโตขึ้นทุกวัน สันติและอุษาตั้งชื่อมันว่า 'น้ำตาล'

เจ้าน้ำตาลเป็นแมวขี้อ้อน เห็นใครอยู่ใกล้ๆ ก็ชอบไปคลอเคลีย

ทุกคนชอบแมวตัวนี้มาก

Reference: ขัณธ์ชัย อธิเกียรติ, รศ.ดร. สิริพัชร์ เจษฎาวิโรจน์, นางเรณู ทวีนันท์. ภาษาไทย วรรณคดีและวรรณกรรม
ป.๖. กรุงเทพฯ : อักษรเจริญทัศน์ อจท. จำกัด, ... (หน้า ๔๔-๔๕)

Translation

Write Down and Then Remember

Two weeks ago aunty Nut (Nút), Santi's (Săn-tì) aunt, brought a Wi-chian-mas (Wí-chiian-mât) species kitten that she got from her friend to give to Santi's (Săn-tì) father. She cannot take care of it because she has changed her work and moved to a new place. Her new place is a condo and animals are not allowed there. This is because those animals might annoy the people who live there.

Santi (Săn-tì) and Usa (Ù-săa) are very excited that they are going to have their own pet. Their parents think that taking care of a pet will make the children have good hearts, kindness, sympathy, and it will also teach them to have responsibility. Therefore, they decided to let Santi (Săn-tì) and Usa (Ù-săa) take care of the kitten.

The kitten is growing up every day. Santi (Săn-tì) and Usa (Ù-săa) named it 'Nam-tan' (Nám-dtaan). It is affectionate. When it sees someone around, it always rubs against them. Everyone likes this cat.

Other Reading Resources

We do realise that some of the reading passages you've just gone through will be way above your level at the moment; but, as we've said many times before, this will change as your vocabulary improves. When this does, your reading comprehension will too.

In Thailand in the 1970's they used to teach children in schools using the มานี - มานะ books and which are now available on the Internet. These books cover ประถมศึกษา ๑ - ๖ (Prathom-suksa 1 - 6) and are excellent resources to take you further.

There are 12 books in total, 2 at each level; and, by the time you finish these, if you're not fluent, I'll eat my hat! (not literally). As an example, the level 6 books have 229 and 307 pages, respectively, so you'll need a good vocabulary to be capable of reading and understanding them.

I hope you realise that this is the difference between where you are now and where you want to be - practice and more practice. You now know how to read Thai and though I can't remember who said it, "You've just got to get good!"

You can download these excellent books via this URL:

http://www.learnthaialphabet.com/readingresources

Note: you will need to create an account and login to get them, but it's free. If you already have the app, you can access this through the members' area.

Also within this package is a book by Hugh Leong, called *A Field Guide to Reading Thai Roadside Signs* and this book holds no surprises from the title giveaway.

It shows you what you will see when you're out and about in Thailand and also presents another problem when reading Thai - different fonts! It can be confusing, but is something you'll encounter and which, as always, requires a little practice.

Websites

There are other websites where you can get other reading resources, some are good, but some aren't quite so great. I don't really like putting links to external websites as these can, and do, frequently change. When I locate additional resources, I will post the links on the above page and email you that the page has been updated.

Appendices

Appendix A - Full List of Thai Consonants

Table A.1 shows a complete list of consonant, their transliterated text names, meaning in Thai, and their initial and their final consonant sounds:

Table A.1. - Full List of Consonants and Names

No.	Thai Character	Transliterated Text Name	Meaning	Initial Consonant Sound	Final Consonant Sound	Consonant Class
1	ก ไก่	Gɔɔ Gài	Chicken	/g/	/k/	Middle
2	ข ไข่	Kɔ̌ɔ Kài	Egg	/k/		High
3	ฃ ขวด	Kɔ̌ɔ Kùat	Bottle	Obsolete		High
4	ค ควาย	Kɔɔ Kwaai	Buffalo	/k/		Low
5	ฅ คน	Kɔɔ Kon	Person	Obsolete		Low
6	ฆ ระฆัง	Kɔɔ Rá-kang	Bell	/k/		Low
7	ง งู	Ngɔɔ Nguu	Snake	/ng/		Low
8	จ จาน	Jɔɔ Jaan	Plate	/j/	/t/	Middle
9	ฉ ฉิ่ง	Chɔ̌ɔ Chìng	Cymbals	/ch/	/t/	High
10	ช ช้าง	Chɔɔ Cháang	Elephant	/ch/	/t/	Low
11	ซ โซ่	Sɔɔ Sôo	Chain	/s/	/t/	Low
12	ฌ เฌอ	Chɔɔ Chəə	Tree	/ch/	/t/	Low
13	ญ หญิง	Yɔɔ Yǐng	Woman	/y/	/n/	Low
14	ฎ ชฎา	Dɔɔ Chá-daa	Head-dress	/d/	/t/	Middle
15	ฏ ปฏัก	Dtɔɔ Bpà-dtàk	Spear	/dt/	/t/	Middle
16	ฐ ฐาน	Tɔ̌ɔ Tǎan	Pedestal	/t/		High
17	ฑ มณโท	Tɔɔ Montoo	Giant's Wife	/t/		Low
18	ฒ ผู้เฒ่า	Tɔɔ Pûu-tâo	Old Man	/t/		Low
19	ณ เณร	Nɔɔ Neen	Monk	/n/		Low
20	ด เด็ก	Dɔɔ Dèk	Child	/d/	/t/	Middle
21	ต เต่า	Dtɔɔ Dtào	Turtle	/dt/	/t/	Middle

Table A.1. - Full List of Consonants and Names

22	ถ ถุง	Tɔ̌ɔ Tǔng	Bag	/t/		High
23	ท ทหาร	Tɔɔ Tá-hǎan	Soldier	/t/		Low
24	ธ ธง	Tɔɔ Tong	Flag	/t/		Low
25	น หนู	Nɔɔ Nǔu	Mouse	/n/		Low
26	บ ใบไม้	Bɔɔ Bai-mái	Leaf	/b/	/p/	Middle
27	ป ปลา	Bpɔɔ Bplaa	Fish	/bp/	/p/	Middle
28	ผ ผึ้ง	Pɔ̌ɔ Pǔng	Bee	/p/		High
29	ฝ ฝา	Fɔ̌ɔ Fǎa	Lid	/f/	/p/	High
30	พ พาน	Pɔɔ Paan	Tray	/p/		Low
31	ฟ ฟัน	Fɔɔ Fan	Tooth	/f/	/p/	Low
32	ภ สำเภา	Pɔɔ Sǎmpao	Junk	/p/		Low
33	ม ม้า	Mɔɔ Máa	Horse	/m/		Low
34	ย ยักษ์	Yɔɔ Yák	Giant	/y/	/i/	Low
36	ร เรือ	Rɔɔ Rɯɯa	Boat	/r/	/n/	Low
36	ล ลิง	Lɔɔ Ling	Monkey	/l/	/n/	Low
37	ว แหวน	Wɔɔ Wɛ̌ɛn	Ring	/w/	/o/	Low
38	ศ ศาลา	Sɔ̌ɔ Sǎa-laa	Tent	/s/	/t/	High
39	ษ ฤๅษี	Sɔ̌ɔ Rɯɯ-sǐi	Hermit	/s/	/t/	High
40	ส เสือ	Sɔ̌ɔ Sɯɯa	Tiger	/s/	/t/	High
41	ห หีบ	Hɔ̌ɔ Hìip	Chest	/h/		High
42	ฬ จุฬา	Lɔɔ Jù-laa	Star-shaped Kite	/l/	/n/	Low
43	อ อ่าง	ɔɔ Àang	Bowl	/ɔɔ/		Middle
44	ฮ นกฮูก	Hɔɔ Nók-hûuk	Owl	/h/		Low

Appendix B - Full List of Vowels

Table B.1 and Table B.2 show the complete list of simple and complex vowels:

Table B.1. - Simple Vowels

Short Vowel			Long Vowel		
Vowel	**Sound**	**Sounds Like**	**Vowel**	**Sound**	**Sounds Like**
The 4 vowels to the right can be short or long but are considered long for tone purposes.			-ำ	/am/	**um**brella
			ใ-	/ai/	k**ni**ght
			ไ-	/ai/	**fly**
			เ-า	/ao/	m**ou**se
-ะ	/a/	p**u**ffin	-า	/aa/	p**a**lm
-ิ	/i/	l**i**p	-ี	/i/	st**ee**ple
-ึ	/ʉ/	p**u**sh-up	-ื	/ʉʉ/	bl**oo**m
-ุ	/u/	cr**oo**k	-ู	/uu/	b**oo**t
เ-ะ	/e/	n**e**t	เ-	/ee/	b**e**d
แ-ะ	/ɛ/	tr**a**p	แ-	/ɛɛ/	**ma**re
โ-ะ	/o/	c**o**t	โ-	/oo/	gh**o**st
เ-าะ	/ɔ/	sl**o**t	-อ	/ɔɔ/	**aw**ful

Table B.2. - Complex Vowels

Short Vowel			Long Vowel		
Vowel	**Sound**	**Sounds Like**	**Vowel**	**Sound**	**Sounds Like**
เ-อะ	/ə/	**a**bove	เ-อ	/əə/	**ear**ly
เ-ียะ	/ia/	**ria**	เ-ีย	/iia/	re**ind**eer
เ-ือะ	/ʉa/	n**ewer**	เ-ือ	/ʉʉa/	sk**ua**
-ัวะ	/ua/	b**uat**	-ัว	/uua/	**pure**
ฤ	/rʉ/	**rook**	ฤๅ	/rʉʉ/	**root**
ฦ	/lʉ/	**loo**kout	ฦๅ	/lʉʉ/	**loo**ney

Appendix C - Classifiers

Classifiers are used quite extensively in language and are used to 'group' objects together. For example, in English we use *herd* as a group classifier for certain animals, including elephants, cattle, etc.; and, Thai is the same: a group of elephants is called โขลง (klŏong).

However, in Thai, group classifiers are much less common and to be able to communicate on a daily basis, you need to know the classifiers for single objects. There are two general form for using classifiers in Thai: noun without an adjective, and noun with an adjective.

Appendix C1 - Noun Without Adjective

When there is no adjective with the noun, this form is used:

noun + number + classifier

Example 1

Rɔɔ Han

Refer to "Rɔɔ Hăn" on page 334 for an explanation of รร.

ผู้ชายคนนั้นมีภรรยาสามคน

noun + number + classifier

(ภรรยา)   (สาม)   (คน)

That man has 3 wives.

Example 2

มีบ้านสิบหลังบนถนนนี้

noun + number + classifier

(บ้าน)   (สิบ)   (หลัง)

There are 10 houses in this street.

Appendix C2 - Noun With Adjective

When an adjective is needed, the following form is used:

noun + adjective + number + classifier

Example 1

ผมเอาเบียร์ใหญ่สามขวดครับ

noun + adjective + number + classifier

(เบียร์)   (ใหญ่)   (สาม)   (ขวด)

I want 3 large bottles of beer please.

Example 2

ผมเห็นหมาสีดำสองตัว

noun +   adjective + number + classifier

(หมา)   (สีดำ)   (สอง)   (ตัว)

I can see 2 black dogs.

Appendix C3 - Common Classifiers

There are hundreds of classifiers in Thai, but here are a few of the common ones:

- บาน – for windows, doors, picture frames, mirrors

- ฉบับ – for letters, newspapers

- แก้ว – for drinking glasses, tumblers

- ใบ – for empty glasses

- ต้น – for trees, plants
- ตัว – for animals, insects, fish, tables and chairs, shirts, pants, coats, other living creatures
- ดวง – for stars, postage stamps
- ฟอง – for poultry eggs
- กลัก – for matchboxes
- ก้อน – for lumps of sugar, stones
- ห่อ – for bundles, parcels
- คน – for a person, a child, human beings
- คู่ – for pairs of articles, e.g. husband and wife, fork and spoon, etc.
- เครื่อง – for electrical appliances: TVs, computers, phones, stereos, etc.
- เล่ม – for books, candles, scissors
- ลำ – for boats, ships, aeroplanes
- เม็ด – for smaller things, fruit pits, pills
- มวน – for cigarettes
- แผ่น – for sheets of paper, planks of wood
- องค์ – for holy personages, kings and monks
- เรือน – for clocks, watches
- รูป – for monks and novices, also for pictures
- สาย – for roads, waterways, belts, etc.
- ซอง – for envelopes
- ถ้วย – for cups
- อัน – for small objects, things (in general) – this is the 'catch-all' classifier if you can't remember the actual one.
- วง – for rings, bracelets, a circle.

Appendix D - Other Language Notes

Appendix D1 - Rɔɔ Hăn

When reading Thai script, you will occasionally see ร (ร เรือ) written twice, e.g. สรรพ or ภรรยา; this combination is called Rɔɔ Hăn.

- When Rɔɔ Hăn is in the medial position and has a final consonant - as in สรรพ - it is pronounced /**a**/ (สรรพ (sàp) means *all, whole, entire*).

- When it is in the final position - as in ภรรยา - it is pronounced /**an**/ (this word is paan-rá-yaa and is yet another example where the final consonant of one syllable ภรรยา becomes the initial consonant of the next). It is a formal way of saying *wife*, e.g. ภรรยาของผม - 'wife of mine' = *my wife*

Appendix D2 - Tɔɔ & Rɔɔ

Low Class ท (Tɔɔ Tá-hăan) never forms a consonant cluster, but there are 17 words in Thai where it is combined with ร เรือ (Rɔɔ Ruua) to form the /**s**/ sound. This /**s**/ sounds comes from ซ โซ่ - Sɔɔ Sôo. We write this combination as ท+ร = ซ.

The easiest way to remember this is: **Tɔɔ + Rɔɔ = Sɔɔ** (or /**t**/+/**r**/ = /**s**/).

These 17 words are:

- ฉะเชิงเทรา – a Thai province
- ทรวง – *chest, breast*
- ทรวดทรง – *shape, contour*
- ทรัพย์ – *wealth, property, estate*
- ทราบ – *know* (formal)
- ทราม – *low, inferior*

- ทราย – *sand*

- ทรุด – *sink*

- เทริด – *crown*

- แทรก – *insert*

- โทรม – *shabby, worn out*

- ไทร – *Banyan Tree*

- นนทรี – *type of tree*

- พุทรา – *type of fruit*

- มัทรี – *Mát-sii* - (a girl's name)*

- อินทรี – *eagle*

* If you look closely at this example, you see how ท provides the final conso-

nant sound of the first syllable, and then combines with ร to form the /t/ + /r/ = /s/ combination as the initial consonant of the second syllable. You don't often see this combination.

Appendix E - Preceding Consonants

A preceding consonant is where a silent and a spoken consonant are joined together to form a single sound; this differs from a consonant cluster where two consonants are joined together and they both produce sound (refer to "Consonant Clusters").

If you have read the section on silent consonants you will understand their role is to 'help' Low Class syllables or words to make, or form, the *low tone* sound – that's what silent consonants do, it's their sole purpose. One thing is, it only happens with certain Low Class consonants, not all of them.

As we know, there are 24 Low Class consonants in total and, if you look at Table 2, you will see that some Low Class consonants make exactly the same sounds as High Class consonants (but have a different tone). They have what are called *equivalent sounds* and are known as **equivalent sound consonants**. These are:

คฅฆชฌฑฒทธพฟภฮ

For example, the first 3 consonants in that list all make the /**k**/ sound (the same as High Class consonants ข and ฃ), the next 2 consonants make the /**ch**/ sound (the same as ฉ), and so on.

In contrast, the remaining Low Class consonants do not have an equivalent High Class consonant sound, they only have a single sound. There are 10 of them and these consonants are known as **single sound consonants**. These are:

งญณนมยรลวฬ

The actual rules are:

1. If อ or ห precede a *single sound consonant,* then neither อ nor ห is pronounced but their respective consonant classes are used to calculate the syllable or word tone (they are both silent).

   For example:

   – อยู่ (yùu)

   – อยาก (yàak)

   – หยด (yòt)

   As we've said before, their purpose is to create a *low tone* sound.

2. If a High Class consonant *precedes* a *single sound consonant* then the High Class ห is added as a silent consonant before the single sound consonant (it is unwritten and it is silent).

For example:

– สงบ (ส-งบ) becomes ส-หงบ (sà-ngòp)

– สงวน (ส-งวน) becomes ส-หงวน (sà-ngǔuan).

3. If a Middle Class consonant *precedes* a *single sound consonant*, High Class consonant ห is added as a silent consonant before the single sound consonant. For example:

– ตลาด (ต-ลาด) becomes ต-หลาด (dtà-làat)

– ตลก (ต-ลก) becomes ต-หลก (dtà-lòk)

Adapted from:http://www.tkl.ac.th/
    index.php?link=general_menu&id_sub=164&na1=หลักการอ่านออกเสียงอักษรนำ

Appendix F - Silent อ

Bearing in mind what has already been covered in the section on Silent Consonants (page 33) and Appendix E (page 335), with Middle Class อ อ่าง, it's purpose is to provide a low tone sound; and, it is helpful to know there are only 4 words which have it as the preceding consonant:

• อย่า – *do not, don't, never*

• อยู่ – *to be at [somewhere], to live at, to stay;* or, it is used to put the verb in the present continuous tense, which shows the action is currently taking place

• อย่าง – *way, sort, variety*; or, it converts an adjective to an adverb (in the same way as adding the suffix –*ly* does in English)

- อยาก – *to want*

Of course, there are far more words which use preceding High Class ห.

Appendix G - Modifying Vowels

Though there are 32 vowels in the Thai alphabet, you will also encounter other variations of these vowels during your Thai studies. These variations are called *modified forms*. There are effectively 3 forms for vowels:

1. *Maintained form* - this is the original form of the vowels, as shown in table Table 5, Full List of Simple Vowels, on page 19 and Table 6, Full List of Complex Vowels, on page 20.

2. *Changed form* - certain vowels can be changed if a final consonant is present.

3. *Reduced form* - effectively shortening the vowel (such as using ็-).

We will look at the changed and reduced form below.

Appendix G1 - Changed Form

The changed form can be applied if the following vowels สระ -ะ, เ-ะ, แ-ะ or เ-อ are followed by the following consonants: ง, น, ด, บ, ม, or ก. For example:

- จะ with the addition of บ becomes จับ

- เตะ with the addition of ม becomes เต็ม

- แขะ with the addition of ง becomes แข็ง

- เงอ with the addition of น becomes เงิน.

Appendix G2 - Reduced Form

If you worked through the book before reading this part of the appendix, you will have encountered practically all of the reduced forms of the vowels, such as the unwritten vowels, Mái Hăn-aa-ġaat, สระ -ว as a medial vowel, etc., but here they are spelled out:

- สระ เ-าะ can be reduced (and replaced) with ็ and สระ อ if the word has a final consonant, e.g.

  - ล + เ-าะ + ก = ล็อก
  - ก + เ-าะ + -อ้ = ก็

Note: as we said in the main text, ก is the one exception which does not need สระ -อ.

- สระ -ะ can be reduced to unwritten vowel /**a**/ (refer to page 57).

- สระ โ-ะ can be reduced to unwritten vowel /**o**/ (refer to page 57).

- สระ -อ can be reduced to an unwritten vowel /**ɔɔ**/ when it follows บ ใบไม้ (refer to page 62).

- สระ -ว can be reduced when it has a final consonant, e.g. รวย (refer to page 279).

- สระ เ-อ can be reduced when it is followed by final consonant ย, e.g. เนย.[8]

As you can see, apart from the last item, you've encountered and are familiar with all of the other reduced forms while working through the book.

---

8. You will note that สระ เ-อ can be found in both changed and reduced form.

Appendix H - Thai Grammar Resources

Though we cover enough grammar in this book to get you started, we only cover a small amount. If you really want to take your reading and your language learning further then there are resources available that can assist.

The following are the only 2 grammar sources that we would recommend:

1. *Thai: An Essential Grammar* (Routledge Essential Grammars) by David Smyth. ISBN: 978-0415226141

2. *Thai Reference Grammar* by James Higbie. ISBN: 978-9748304960

The main problem with these books is neither of them use the Paiboon transliteration system. It is awkward, but if you are at the point where you can read Thai script (or at the point where you don't let the transliteration used distract you), then they will be useful

If you do decide to get the Smyth book from Amazon, you will notice that it's also available on the Kindle. Our recommendation to you is to check this out first, as it used to be just images of the book converted into Kindle format and may not be exactly what you're looking for (January 2014).

Answers to Exercises

Answers to Exercise 1 (page 41)

Exercise 1a:

1) *low tone;* 2) *falling tone;* 3) *falling tone;* 4) *falling tone;* 5) *low tone;* 6) *high tone;* 7) *falling tone;* 8) *high tone;* 9) *low tone.*

Exercise 1b:

- If a syllable ends with a **short** vowel, or it ends with a **stop** final consonant, it is a dead syllable.
- If a syllable ends with a **long** vowel, or it ends with a **sonorant** final consonant, it is a **live** syllable.

Exercise 1c:

1) *mid tone (**MLM**),* 2) *low tone (**HDL**),* 3) *mid tone (**MLM**),* 4) *mid tone (**LLMH**),* 5) *high tone (**LDSH**),* 6) *falling tone (**LDLF**),* 7) *rising tone (**HLR**),* 8) *low tone (**MDL**).*

Answers to Exercise 2 (page 63)

Exercise 2a:

1. With only 2 consonants, there can only be 1 syllable, so rule 7 applies and the vowel is unwritten /**o**/. When a verb, it means *to coil, to curl up, to twist;* and, when a noun, it means *coil, ring, circle.*

---

2. We covered this earlier and it's the same as answer 1: there is only 1 syllable so it has to be unwritten /**o**/. บน is a preposition and means *on*.

3. There are 2-syllables. The unwritten vowel is actually between the initial consonant พ and the initial consonant of the second syllable พ**นั**ก. As the consonants are in different syllables, rule 8 applies, and the unwritten vowel is /**a**/.

4. If there are only 2 consonants it has to be a single syllable word and the unwritten vowel has to be /**o**/. จด means *to jot down, to note*.

5. Similar to the previous example, rule 7 applies and the unwritten vowel is /**o**/. จน means *poor, penniless, impoverished.*

6. Rule 7 applies and the word ดง means *jungle, thick grove* (/**o**/).

7. There is a consonant cluster here and the กล is treated a single consonant. This means there are effectively only 2 consonants in this single syllable word (กล and ม), and rule 7 applies (/**o**/). กลม means *round, circular.*

8. There is also a consonant cluster here (พร), with ม as the final consonant. As they are in the same syllable, rule 7 applies again, and the unwritten vowel is /**o**/. พรม means *carpet, rug* as a noun; and *to sprinkle, to spray,* as a verb.

Exercise 2b:

1. ขด - **High Class + Dead** syllable = *low tone* (**HDL**) = kòt

2. บน - **Middle Class + Live** syllable = *mid tone* (**MLM**) = bon

3. ฉลาด

   – Syllable 1: **High Class + Dead** syllable = *low tone* (**HDL**) = chà

– Syllable 2: **H**igh Class + **D**ead syllable a= *low tone* (HDL) = làat

= chà-làat

4. จด - **M**iddle Class + **D**ead syllable = *low tone* (MDL) = jòt

5. จน - **M**iddle Class + **L**ive syllable = *mid tone* (MLM) = jon

6. ดง - **M**iddle Class + **L**ive syllable = *mid tone* (MLM) = dong

7. กลม - **M**iddle Class + **L**ive syllable = *mid tone* (MLM) = glom

8. พรม - **L**ow Class + **L**ive syllable = *mid tone* (LLM)

Answers to Exercise 3 (page 76)

Exercise 3a:

1e; 2a; 3c (or g); 4f; 5d; 6b; 7g (or c).

Exercise 3b:

1) กะ|ว่า; 2) ประ|เทศ; 3) กระ|ดาน; 4) ระ|บบ; 5) ทะ|เล; 6) สะ|บัด.

Exercise 3c:

1) *low tone (HDL)*, 2) *high tone (LDSH)*, 3) *low tone (MDL)*, 4) *mid tone, (LLM)*, 5) *mid tone (MLM)*, 6) *rising tone (HLR)*, 7) *low tone, (MDL)*, 8) *low tone (HDL)*, 9) *mid tone (LLM)*.

Answers to Exercise 4 (page 87)

Exercise 4a:

1i; 2m; 3f; 4d; 5l; 6b; 7k; 8a; 9e; 10g; 11h; 12j; 13c.

Exercise 4b:

1) กำ|จัด; 2) ทำ|งาน; 3) สำ|หรับ; 4) นำ|เข้า; 5) ทำ|งาน|ทำ|การ; 6) นำ|ไป|ใช้.

Answers to Exercise 5 (page 101)

Exercise 5a

1c; 2f; 3l; 4g; 5h; 6n; 7j; 8d; 9m; 10b: 11e; 12a; 13k;14i.

Exercise 5b

1) ชำ|นาญ; 2) ทำ|ลาย; 3) น้ำ|แข็ง; 4) รัก|ษา; 5) น้ำ|มัน; 6) สะ|พาน.

Answers to Exercise 6 (page 113)

Exercise 6a

1g; 2k; 3j; 4m; 5i; 6l; 7n; 8f; 9a; 10e: 11o; 12d; 13c;14h; 15b.

Exercise 6b

1) จำ|เป็น; 2) ประ|มาณ; 3) เมต|ตา; 4) เม|ล็ด; 5) ระ|หว่าง; 6) รับ|ประ|ทาน; 7) ราง|วัล;

8) รู้|จัก; 9) สำ|นึก.

Answers to Exercise 7 (page 125)

Exercise 7a

1f; 2i; 3l; 4o; 5h; 6j; 7n; 8m; 9b; 10d: 11a; 12c; 13e;14k; 15g.

Exercise 7b

1) แข็ง|แรง; 2) แล้ว|แต่; 3) แทน|ที่; 4) แม้|แต่; 5) แทบ|จะ; 6) แทน|ที่|จะ; 7) แนะ|นำ;

8) แผ่น|ดิน; 9) แพง|มาก.

Answers to Exercise 8 (page 144)

Exercise 8a

1m; 2g; 3j; 4c; 5o; 6i; 7k; 8l; 9a; 10n: 11h; 12b; 13f; 14e; 15d.

Exercise 8b

1) กำ|ไร; 2) ภาย|ใน; 3) เมื่อ|ไร; 4) เสีย|ใจ; 5) ไป|จาก; 6) ตอน|ใต้; 7) ไล่|ล่า; 8) ใย|แก้ว;

9) ใน|ใจ.

Answers to Exercise 9 (page 159)

Exercise 9a

1k; 2d; 3m; 4j; 5n; 6i; 7l; 8o; 9h; 10f: 11c; 12a; 13g;14e; 15b.

Exercise 9b

1) เท่า|ไร; 2) เกา|หลี; 3) เก้า|แสน; 4) เช้า|มืด; 5) เข้า|มา; 6) เงา|มืด; 7) เก่า|แก่; 8) เช่า|ซื้อ; 9)
เช้าวันนี้.

Answers to Exercise 10 (page 173)

Exercise 10a

1f; 2o; 3i; 4e; 5l; 6h; 7a; 8b; 9n; 10c; 11g; 12k; 13j;14m; 15d.

Exercise 10b

1) กิ|ริ|ยา; 2) ค|ดี; 3) ชี|วิต; 4) ญี่|ปุ่น; 5) ตัด|สิน; 6) นิ|ยม; 7) กิ|เลส; 8) นา|พิ|กา;

9) พิ|พิธ|ภัณฑ์.

Answers to Exercise 11 (page 192)

Exercise 11a

1e; 2a; 3o; 4i; 5l; 6n; 7d; 8j; 9b; 10k; 11h; 12f; 13g;14c; 15m.

Exercise 11b

1) วัน|ศุกร์; 2) รู้|สึก; 3) ม|นุษย์; 4) ประ|ตู; 5) ประ|ชุม; 6) บุ|หรี่; 7) ครู|ฝึก; 8) ดู|เหมือน;

9) มิ|ถุ|นา|ยน.

Answers to Exercise 12 (page 205)

Exercise 12a

1l; 2i; 3f; 4g; 5m; 6o; 7j; 8e; 9a; 10b; 11d; 12h; 13k;14c; 15n.

Exercise 12b

1) ชื่อ|เล่น; 2) ข้า|ศึก; 3) พึ่ง|พา; 4) ซื้อ|ขาย; 5) ฝึก|หัด; 6) หรือ|เปล่า; 7) พื้น|ที่; 8) มือ|ถือ;

9) สื่อ|สาร.

Answers to Exercise 13 (page 217)

Exercise 13a

1c; 2i; 3m; 4a; 5k; 6l; 7d; 8b; 9o; 10j; 11e; 12f; 13h;14g; 15n.

Exercise 13b

1) ชั่ว|โมง; 2) โบ|ราณ; 3) ประ|โยชน์; 4) โรง|เรียน; 5) สิง|โต; 6) โอ|กาส; 7) โกรธ|ง่าย; 8)

โม|ท|นา; 9) ความ|โก|ลา|หล.

Answers to Exercise 14 (page 227)

Exercise 14a

1d; 2e; 3a; 4k; 5m; 6b; 7i; 8g; 9f; 10l; 11n; 12c; 13o;14j; 15h.

Exercise 14b

The hidden vowel is highlighted **bold**.

1. สงสัย

- Syllable 1: **H**igh Class + **L**ive syllable = *rising tone* (**HLR**) = sǒng
- Syllable 2: **H**igh Class + **L**ive syllable = *rising tone* (**HLR**) = sǎi

$$= \text{sǒng-sǎi} \ (suspicious)$$

2. ฉบับ

- Syllable 1: **H**igh Class + **D**ead syllable = *low tone* (**HDL**) = chà
- Syllable 2: **H**igh Class + **D**ead syllable = *low tone* (**HDL**) = bàp

$$= \text{chà-bàp} \ (copy, \ issue, \ edition, \ \text{and}$$
is the classifier for documents letters, papers, newspapers)

3. จดหมาย

- Syllable 1: **M**iddle Class + **D**ead syllable = *low tone* (**MDL**) = jòt
- Syllable 2: **H**igh Class + **L**ive syllable = *rising tone* (**HLR**) = maǎi

$$= \text{jòt-mǎi} \ (letter, \ correspondence, \ mail)$$

4. มนุษย์

- Syllable 1: **L**ow Class + **D**ead syllable and **S**hort vowel = *high tone* (**LDSH**) = má
- Syllable 2: **L**ow Class + **D**ead syllable and **S**hort vowel = *high tone* (**LDSH**) = nút

= má-nút (*human, human being*)

5. ชนิด

- Syllable 1: Low Class + **D**ead syllable and **S**hort vowel = *high tone* (**LDSH**) = chá
- Syllable 2: Low Class + **D**ead syllable and **S**hort vowel = *high tone* (**LDSH**) = nít

= chá-nít (*type, kind, sort*; and, it's a classifier for type, sort or kind of something)

6. ประชาชน

- Syllable 1: **M**iddle Class + **D**ead syllable = *low tone* (**MDL**) = bprà
- Syllable 2: **L**ow Class + **L**ive syllable = *mid tone* (**LLM**) = chaa
- Syllable 3: **L**ow Class + **L**ive syllable = *mid tone* (**LLM**) = chon

= bprà-chaa-chon (*people, inhabitants, residents*)

Answers to Exercise 15 (page 240)

Exercise 15a

1l; 2k; 3d; 4i; 5b; 6a; 7j; 8m; 9g; 10o; 11e; 12n; 13c; 14h; 15f.

Exercise 15b

1) เกาะ|ส|มุย; 2) เกาะ|กลาง; 3) เพาะ|ชำ; 4) เพราะ|ฉะ|นั้น; 5) เจาะ|จง|ชื่อ; 6) เพาะ|เลี้ยง|สัตว์|น้ำ.

Answers to Exercise 16 (page 253)

Exercise 16a

1c; 2g; 3j; 4l; 5b; 6h; 7d; 8a; 9k; 10n; 11m; 12i; 13f; 14o; 15e.

Exercise 16b

1. ส้มตำ - the written สระ ◌ำ clearly identifies the second syllable for us, which leaves ส and ม as the 2 consonants in the first syllable. Rule 7 tells us unwritten /o/ is between 2 consonants in the same syllable. For tone:

   − Syllable 1: High Class + Mái too = *falling tone*

   − Syllable 2: **M**iddle Class + **L**ive syllable = *mid tone* (MLM)

   ส้มตำ = sôm-dtam (papaya salad)

2. ขนาด - long vowel สระ -า is the medial vowel between Low Class น and the final consonant. This means that the initial consonant, High Class ข, is on its own at the front and rule 8 tells us that unwritten /a/ comes between 2 consonants in different syllables.

   − Syllable 1: **H**igh Class + **D**ead syllable = *low tone* (HDL)

   − Syllable 2: Don't forget the preceding consonant rule here ("Preceding Consonants" on page 335). **H**igh Class + **D**ead syllable = *low tone* (**HDL**)

   ขนาด = kà-nàat (dimensions, size, measurement)

3. ถวาย - we can see our written long vowel สระ -า here again. We know ว can be the second consonant in a number of consonant clusters but does it form clusters with High Class ถ? The answer is no. Therefore, ว is the initial consonant of the second syllable and rule 8 applies. For tone, syllable 1 is the same as in the previous example, but again we have a *single sound consonant* (ว) as the initial consonant of the second syllable, so:

   − Syllable 1: **H**igh Class + **D**ead syllable = *low tone* (**HDL**)

   − Syllable 2: **H**igh Class + **L**ive syllable = *rising tone* (**HLR**)

   ถวาย = tà-wăai (to give, to offer, to present)

4. ทหาร - if you got the last question correct, example 4 follows <u>exactly</u> the same process for the unwritten vowel.

ทหาร = tá-hǎan (soldier)

5. บริการ - this word has 3 syllables and after we identify the 2 written vowels. We see the second consonant is very often seen as the second consonant in consonant clusters; and, as it has a written vowel above it, it also means it's following the written vowel/cluster rule. The question is, do บ and ร form consonant clusters? A quick glance at Table 3 on page 16 shows us they don't and they must therefore be in separate syllables: rule 8.

Do you remember back to "Quirk with /ɔɔ/" on page 62, which states that when the initial consonant of a syllable is บ the unwritten vowel is pronounced /ɔɔ/ and not /a/? This is one of those examples. The tone is:

— Syllable 1: **M**iddle Class + **L**ive syllable = *mid tone* (MLM)

— Syllable 2: **L**ow Class + **D**ead syllable and **S**hort vowel = *high tone* (LDSH)

— Syllable 3: **M**iddle Class + **L**ive syllable = *mid tone* (MLM)

บริการ = bɔɔ-rí-gaan (service)

6. ถนน - with ถนน, if the first 2 consonants (ถ and น) belong to the same syllable, then the unwritten vowel will be /o/ (/t/ + /o/ + /n/). This then means that the middle consonant (-น-) would be the final consonant of the first syllable (ถน-) and the initial consonant of the second syllable (-นน); and, as it is the final consonant of the first syllable it would be in a different syllable to the final น. The problem is, unwritten /a/ is actually สระ -ะ. If you remember that this vowel is always written after a consonant and that rule 5 states that สระ -ะ always marks the end of a syllable, this would leave the second น 'dangling' at the end of the syllable without a vowel. This is not allowed so it can't be right.

Therefore, น and น have to be in the same syllable, which means rule 7, unwritten /o/, applies. As this then leaves ถ on it's own at the beginning of the word, it must be in a different syllable and rule 8, unwritten /a/, applies. Remember the preceding consonant rules here.

- Syllable 1: **H**igh Class + **D**ead syllable = *low tone* (**HDL**)

- Syllable 2: **H**igh Class + **L**ive syllable = *rising tone* (**HLR**)

ถนน = tà-nŏn (*street, road*)

Answers to Exercise 17 (page 266)

Exercise 17a

1h; 2e; 3f; 4k; 5m; 6b; 7g; 8j; 9l; 10a; 11n; 12c; 13d; 14o; 15i.

Exercise 17b

1) ตะ|เกียง; 2) เลี้ยว|ซ้าย; 3) เทียบ|เคียง; 4) เกียจ|คร้าน; 5) เกี่ยว|ข้อง; 6) เพียง|อย่าง|เดียว;

7) นัก|เรียน|ประ|ถม; 8) โต๊ะ|เขียน|หนัง|สือ; 9) กระ|ดาษ|เขียน|หนัง|สือ.

Answers to Exercise 18 (page 276)

Exercise 18a

1d; 2c; 3m; 4g; 5h; 6i; 7k; 8b; 9j; 10f; 11a; 12n; 13e;14o; 15l.

Exercise 18b

1) เกือบ|จะ ; 2) เครือ|ข่าย; 3) เดือน|ก่อน; 4) เคือง|ใจ; 5) พ่อ|เมือง; 6) เตือน|ส|ติ;

7) เนื่อง|มา|จาก; 8) เพื่อน|ร่วม|งาน; 9) สำ|นัก|งาน|ตรวจ|คน|เข้า|เมือง.

Answers to Exercise 19 (page 287)

Exercise 19a

1d; 2c; 3f; 4e; 5g; 6k; 7o; 8a; 9j; 10n; 11b; 12l; 13i; 14h; 15m.

Exercise 19b

1) กระ|ทรวง; 2) ต้น|มะ|ม่วง; 3) ขวด|นม; 4) จำ|นวน; 5) ช|นวน; 6) ช่วย|งาน;

7) ควร|ป|ฏิ|บัต; 8) ดวง|วิญ|ญาณ; 9) ปวง|ชน|ชาว|ไทย.

References

Higbie, J., & Thinsan, S. (2008). *Thai Reference Grammar - The Structure of Spoken Thai.*
Bangkok: Orchid Press.

Smyth, D. (2002). *Thai: An Essential Grammae.* Abingdon: Routledge.

Thungkulaphitayakom School. (no date). *หลักการอ่านออกเสียงอักษรนำ.* Retrieved June 6th, 2013,
from Thungkulaphitayakom School: http://www.tkl.ac.th/
index.php?link=general_menu&id_sub=164&na1=หลักการอ่านออกเสียงอักษรนำ

มานพ สอนศิริ, รศ.ดร. สิริพัชร์ เจษฎาวิโรจน์, เฉลา อรุณรัตน์. ภาษาไทย
หลักภาษาและการใช้ภาษา ป.๑. กรุงเทพฯ : อักษรเจริญทัศน์ อจท. จำกัด, .. (หน้า 18)

วีณา วงศ์ศรีเผือก และคณะ. ภาษาไทย ป.๒. กรุงเทพฯ : อักษรเจริญทัศน์ อจท. จำกัด, ๒๕๔๒
(หน้า 14)

มานพ สอนศิริ และคณะ. ภาษาไทย วรรณคดีและวรรณกรรม ป.๓. กรุงเทพฯ : อักษรเจริญทัศน์
อจท. จำกัด, ... (หน้า 44)

เอกรินทร์ สี่มหาศาล และคณะ. ภาษาไทย ป.๔, กรุงเทพฯ : อักษรเจริญทัศน์ อจท. จำกัด, ๒๕๔๓
(หน้า 9)

ขัณธ์ชัย อธิเกียรติ, รศ.ดร. สิริพัชร์ เจษฎาวิโรจน์. ภาษาไทย วรรณคดีและวรรณกรรม ป.๕.
กรุงเทพฯ : อักษรเจริญทัศน์ อจท. จำกัด, ... (หน้า 5)

ขัณธ์ชัย อธิเกียรติ, รศ.ดร. สิริพัชร์ เจษฎาวิโรจน์, นางเรณู ทวีนันท์. ภาษาไทย
วรรณคดีและวรรณกรรม ป.๖. กรุงเทพฯ : อักษรเจริญทัศน์ อจท. จำกัด, ... (หน้า ๔๔-๔๕)

http://www.omg-facts.com/History/The-Real-Name-Of-Bangkok-Is-The-Longest/51705

U

V

W

A Note from the Authors

That's it, you reached the end of the book. First of all, well done; and, second, if you've worked through this book page-by-page, you probably know more about reading Thai than 99.xx% of foreigners (and probably quite a few Thais as well).

Much of the material in this book has only been covered before in Thai language/grammar books and with this foundation, we sincerely hope you're now in a better situation to continue your studies.

Unfortunately, this is where the tuition for this book ends. We hope it has been as great a learning experience for you, the reader, as it has been enjoyable for us, the authors. Above all, we hope that it has set you up for your future, that it has been fun to learn, and your experience with us has been rewarding. When we started on our first book in 2010, we always knew that the journey would be epic; and, indeed, we hope that with our method of learning Thai, this has become another in your list of great adventures.

Best wishes,

Russ and Duangta

p.s. If we have helped you, then please consider helping us. A testimonial for the website, or a review on Amazon (or wherever you bought the book), is the single key deciding factor in persuading those who are unsure of whether or not to take the leap of faith that you yourself did, and if you would be so kind, we'd really appreciate it. It's not required, we're just asking for your help :-).

In addition, if you have feedback, comments, or anything, then please let us know. We do listen – as any of the people who have bought the Learn Thai Alphabet application will tell you – and most updates are as a result of request for improvements. You can always contact us at:

info@learnthaialphabet.com or info@howtoreadthai.com.

Our Other Quest Products

The book that started it all: *Learning Thai, Your Great Adventure.*

ISBN: 978-1-908203-00-7. Published 2nd March 2011. 181 pages.

Memory Aids to Your Great Adventure

ISBN: 978-1-908203-04-5.

Published 22nd December 2011. 50 pages.

The Perfect Thai Phrasebook

ISBN: 978-1-908203-05-2. Published 11th November 2012. 100 pages.

The Learn Thai Alphabet Application

Released 10th March 2013.

Learn the Thai alphabet on your pc, Mac, or iPad. Based on *MATYGA*, you get interactive learning and quizzes, sounds by native speakers and much more. Guided and unguided learning, consonant classes, consonant sounds, vowel sounds, punctuation, tone marks, and numbers. This has to be the quickest and easiest way to learn the Thai alphabet.

Please see overleaf.

- PTO -

A Note from the Authors

The Learn Thai Alphabet Application

Some screenshots from the application showing the interface, consonants, consonant classes, vowels, rockstars (hard) level, tone marks, test results, audio, etc.

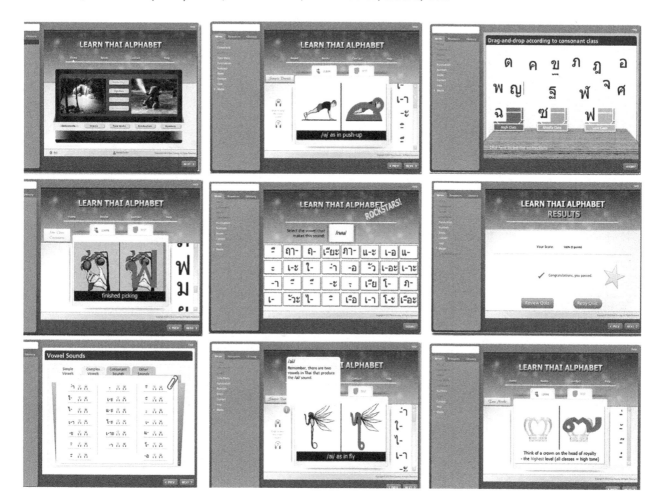

Available from www.learnthaialphabet.com

How to Read Thai Audio Book

The audio book for this book will be available in the second quarter of 2014.

Check the following website for details: www.howtoreadthai.com/audiobook

www.learnthaialphabet.com

Made in United States
Orlando, FL
19 August 2022

21290472R00209